"Nearly twenty years ago, as a father of an adventurous young boy, I received God's mercy through a mysterious messenger. When I share this memory with others, I am often asked, 'Do you think he was an angel?' I never got the chance to ask him. Had he stayed I would have thanked him profusely, but I am reminded of Revelation 22:9 (NAS): 'Do not do that. I am a fellow servant of yours and of your brethren the prophets and of those who heed the words of this book. Worship God.' For me, those words–spoken by an angel and recorded by John–took on a greater depth that fateful day. In my flesh, I could not protect my son. I don't know if there is a more humbling position to be in as a father. My son–still as adventurous as ever–is now a man who serves the Lord, as a pastor, with his whole heart. We are both thrilled to be a part of this book. Cecil and Twila have a passion and a talent for encouraging believers to trust in God. We believe this book will do just that. As you read these fascinating accounts of our *Heavenly Company*, we trust you will join the voices of angels crying out, 'Worship God.'"

Roy Peterson, President, The Seed Company

"Angels are everywhere. If you've ever doubted their existence, all you need do is read these true life accounts from those who have encountered these heavenly beings. Their stories will inspire, encourage and touch your heart with the assurance God is willing, ready and able to work in the lives of His children."

–*Debbie Macomber*, The New York Times *Best-selling Author*

D0061350

"If you're looking for a book that will renew your hope, revive your heart and remind you of the supernatural intervention of God in everyday life, this is it! *Heavenly Company* is filled with miraculous stories of people who have experienced the presence of angels in the middle of unexpected challenges, fearful encounters and daily activities. Buy one for yourself and ten to give away. This book will bolster your faith and comfort your soul."

–Carol Kent, Speaker and Author

HEAVENLY COMPANY

ENTERTAINING ANGELS UNAWARE

FROM *THE NEW YORK TIMES* BEST-SELLING AUTHOR

CECIL MURPHEY
AND TWILA BELK

FOREWORD BY DON PIPER

Guideposts
New York, New York

ISBN-10: 0-8249-3170-X
ISBN-13: 978-0-8249-3170-4

Published by Guideposts
16 East 34th Street
New York, New York 10016
Guideposts.org

Acknowledgments

Every attempt has been made to credit the sources of copyrighted material used in this book. If any such acknowledgment has been inadvertently omitted or miscredited, receipt of such information would be appreciated.

Clyde Taylor (1904–1988) was a pioneer missionary in Peru. Carolyn Curtis wrote an account of his life in *A Man for All Nations: The Story of Clyde and Ruth Taylor* (PA: Camp Hill, Christian Publications, Inc.) 1998.

"Bats in Our Belfry" by Terri Elders appeared in a different form in *A Book of Miracles* by Bernie S. Siegel and Deepak Chopra (New York: New World Library), 2011. The author retains reprint rights.

"Ice Water in the Desert" by Helen L. Hoover appeared in slightly different form in Word Aflame Publication, 8-8-2011.

Unless noted, Scripture verses are taken from the *Holy Bible, New Living Translation*, copyright © 1996, 2004. Used by permission of Tyndale House Publishers, Inc., Wheaton, IL. 60189. All rights reserved.

Scripture quotations marked (ESV) are from *The Holy Bible, English Standard Version*® (ESV®), copyright © 2001, ESV Text Edition: 2011, by Crossway, a publishing ministry of Good News Publishers. Used by permission. All rights reserved.

All other stories © Cecil Murphey and Twila Belk. All rights reserved.

Library of Congress Cataloging-in-Publication Data

Murphey, Cecil.
  Heavenly company : entertaining angels unaware / by Cecil Murphey, with Twila Belk.
    p. cm.
  ISBN 978-0-8249-3170-4 (pbk.)
1. Angels–Christianity—Anecdotes. I. Belk, Twila. II. Title.
  BT966.3.M87 2012
  235'.3–dc23

                              2012017013

Cover and interior design by Müllerhaus
Typeset by Aptara, Inc.

Printed and bound in the United States of America
10 9 8 7 6 5 4 3 2 1

CONTENTS

FOREWORD

FEW TOPICS ENGENDER AS much curiosity as extraterrestrials. Reactions to their existence usually fall into two categories: those who are rabid believers and those who believe that believers in extraterrestrials are daft.

Count me among those who believe in ETs. I'm not referring to little green creatures or visitors from distant planets. I submit that we not only have extraterrestrial visitations in our midst, but these messengers, these servants, these protectors, are around us even now. They are the angels of God. *Heavenly Company: Entertaining Angels Unaware* is an exciting and encouraging effort to chronicle encounters with those awesome beings.

Angels are like us, and they are not. We have God the Creator in common. There is evidence that our very likeness can be similar in appearance. Thus, there is the biblical declaration that we might not even know when we are entertaining them (Hebrews 13:2). We may not be aware that they are angels and not human. Angels are at the beck and call of God, and yet their efforts often seem directed toward us. Thank God, that's true. Angels guide, protect, deliver, strengthen, encourage and transport us to heaven at the time of our deaths. Angels tell us things God wants us to know.

This is a book about angelic encounters–God's servants interacting with God's people . . . people like you and me. When you finish reading this book, you may not be looking over your shoulder straining to detect an unseen angel. But we pray that you'll be encouraged to know that angels are all around us. Perhaps in sharing these enlightening stories, we will be more sensitive to the work and closeness of angels.

As you will discover, I held the hand of an angel, one of God's ETs. I believe I live today because I did. Angels aren't winged chubby toddlers playing harps. They're the mighty servants of God. And you might be surprised. Maybe one is just over your shoulder right now.

—Don Piper

INTRODUCTION

In the Company of Angels?

WHO ARE THOSE ANGELS that appear without explanation and often disappear just as mysteriously? Are they human? Spirits in human form?

As you read each story, you'll have to make that decision for yourself. We have no answers, nor an agenda. We've compiled for you here, in this volume, extraordinary tales in response to desperate prayer.

The stories we've chosen have three common elements: the unexpected; the unexplained; awe.

Each of these true accounts takes place at a point of crisis. An urgent need. A moment of desperation. The ordinary people in these real-life stories prayed—and something amazing and life-changing occurred.

As we edited these narratives, one thing continued to stand out to us: The agents of God did their appointed tasks and promptly disappeared.

The stories come from a wide variety of sources and people who don't know each other. And yet the commonality of their experiences makes us believe they were truly in the company of angels. Perhaps they will encourage you to believe in them as well.

✦ ✦ ✦ ✦ ✦

The Hebrew word for angel is *malak*. It means messenger or ambassador. We get the common name Michael from the word. *Malak* refers to someone sent from God for a specific purpose.

The Bible doesn't explain the origin of angels or where they're from. Regarding angels, the book of Hebrews declares, "Angels are only servants–spirits sent to care for people who will inherit salvation" (Hebrews 1:14).

Servants of God. They care for God's people.

That doesn't tell us everything, but isn't it enough?

HEAVENLY COMPANY

CHAPTER ONE

The Man in White

Cecil Murphey

My stomach feels queasy," I said as I drove across the washboard-rutted road in the hot, dry season of equatorial Africa. "And I'm a little nauseated."

"You want to stop? Have me drive?" my wife Shirley asked.

I shook my head and said, "Whatever it is will probably pass." Instead, the queasiness increased and a light, throbbing pain added to my discomfort. I drove our yellow four-cylinder British-made Ford over the rough, red-clay roads of Kenya for almost an hour. My nausea worsened and the pain increased.

For more than four years, our family of five had lived near Lake Victoria in a remote area of Kenya. During all that time, Shirley had battled chronic malaria, and our kids suffered from malaria and a variety of other, unexplained fevers. But I hadn't been sick even once.

About five miles from home, a wave of bile washed up into my throat. I pulled over to the side of the road. Not having time to get out, I leaned over the open window and vomited. Perspiration covered my body and my strength drained away. After a few minutes, I felt slightly better and continued to drive.

Within minutes, I was flushed as if I had a fever, but I sensed my temperature was normal. I pulled into our driveway just as a spasm of pain struck my abdomen. I slammed on the brakes, flung open the door, half fell out of the car, and vomited again. I felt so weak that I could hardly stand up. I leaned against the side of the car until Shirley came around to support my left shoulder.

Despite her outward calmness, Shirley's eyes couldn't hide her deep concern.

"I'll be okay," I whispered.

Shirley didn't believe me. She was headmistress of a girls' dormitory of a Christian mission school. She signaled one of the teenaged girls, who raced up the winding path from the cinder-block building. Both of them held me while I slowly took one step after another. I mumbled something about the pain and couldn't figure out why I was sick. I'm one of those people who just doesn't get sick. With their help, I staggered into the house and collapsed on the sofa.

Another roiling of my intestines forced me to vomit once more. This time it was the dry heaves; I had nothing left inside my stomach. The excruciating pain increased. I'd never before felt such physical torment. The dryness of my throat and mouth made me cry out for a drink. "Water, just a little water."

"Are you sure?" my wife asked.

Too weak to talk, I nodded just as pain stabbed me and it felt as if it were ripping my entire abdomen in two.

As soon as the pain eased, Shirley held a glass to my lips. "Slowly," she said.

I sipped perhaps an ounce before a violent spasm forced me to expel the water.

We had arrived home about four o'clock in the afternoon after finishing a two-day seminar for church leaders. Just before Shirley and I left, we ate a large meal with them of millet, rice, and chicken.

Lying in agony, I forgot about the seminar. I hurt and the pain didn't seem to ease. For the next five hours, I lay on the sofa, unable to keep down even a sip of water. Like everyone else in that remote part of the country, we had no electricity, but we did have a kerosene-operated refrigerator. Twice Shirley put ice chips into my mouth, but both times that started a fresh attack of the dry heaves.

Worse than the vomiting, the intestinal pain struck every few minutes. We had no medicine except aspirin. Twice I tried to dissolve one in my mouth, but I couldn't get it down.

We prayed but I didn't get any better. Someone called the local African pastor who prayed for me, but nothing changed. I couldn't lie still and thrashed with each stabbing jolt. No position alleviated the pain, and if I moved too much, the nausea returned.

Finally, weak and unable to keep anything down, I lay quietly and prayed, "God, take away the pain. Please take away my pain." It didn't get better.

About ten o'clock I forced myself to walk into the bedroom. I didn't try to undress but fell across my side of the bed. For over an hour, I lay there as new spasms struck every few minutes. My jerking disturbed Shirley, and I'm not sure she could sleep anyway. Twice she got up and laid a damp cloth on my perspiring forehead.

I took a pillow and blanket and lay on the cement floor. "I'll be all right," I said and told her to go back to sleep.

I stifled my groans as the pains continued. By midnight, I had gotten no better. My parched throat cried out for water, but I feared the vomiting would start again.

Although nausea no longer troubled me, I felt one unrelenting spasm after another. Sharp, stabbing pains wrapped themselves around my entire abdomen and squeezed tightly for maybe half a minute and slowly diminished, only to start again.

We had no telephone and lived more than fifty miles from a tiny, inadequate clinic. The Seventh-Day Adventist hospital was more than a three-hour drive and I didn't have the strength to walk out to the car for Shirley to drive me there.

I lay on the floor, feeling each pain and trying to make no noise to keep from disturbing Shirley. Just then, a light shone into my eyes.

"Oh, God, please, please touch me," I cried out as a stronger spasm hit. The pain intensified and each wave lasted longer. "Please, God, if You care . . ."

The sound of footsteps told me someone was in the room. The person stopped and I looked up. Standing only a foot from me was a man wearing a white suit, but I couldn't make out his features.

The man knelt beside me and laid his hand on my abdomen. Instantly, the pain vanished.

"Thank you," I said. I lay on the floor and gave thanks to God. After a few minutes I got up and crawled into bed next to Shirley. Strange as it may sound, I felt so tired, I could think of nothing but sleep. I fell asleep without trying to figure it out.

A few minutes after six the next morning, the distant ringing of cowbells awakened me. A heavy truck lumbered down the road. Everyone else in the house was still asleep.

Aware that I felt no pain, I thought of what happened during the night. "How did the man in white get inside?" I asked. I jumped out of bed and ran to the front door and then to the back. Both were still dead bolted.

I hadn't hallucinated, of that I was sure. In fact, hallucination would have been a simple explanation. A man in a white suit had come into my room. He had touched me and removed my pain.

I had been under God's protection and I believe a heavenly angel touched me.

CHAPTER TWO

Angel to the Rescue

Lori Hintermeister

Point of Grace concert was a delightful way to end a fun day at the Iowa State Fair. My sister Connie and I, along with our ten-year-old daughters, made the three-hour trip early that morning so we could enjoy a full day of attractions, rides, fried food, and gazing at the famous cow sculpture made of butter.

The hot, sunny weather, typical for Iowa in August, made our day even better. We left the fair tired but content at about eleven that night.

It was sprinkling when we left and soon rain fell steadily. Heavy rains developed into a thunderstorm shortly after we began our trip home, yet our mood remained light as we belted out tunes from the concert and listened to the girls' excited chatter in the backseat of the van.

Thirty minutes into the trip, the van started to wobble and vibrate. Connie pulled on to the side of the highway. "I think we have a flat."

"What are we going to do?" I watched the rain pelt the windshield. "Do you know how to fix a flat?"

The van quivered as an eighteen-wheeler whizzed by, a reminder that we were a few feet from Interstate 80.

"I don't have any idea where the spare and jack are stored. I didn't expect problems with a new van," Connie said.

We considered our predicament. Flat tire. No cell phones. Pouring rain. No nearby buildings. Two young girls in the backseat. Pitch black, except for the occasional flash of lightning and the lights in our van. Sparse traffic other than the semis zooming past us on the Interstate. "What are we going to do?" I asked again, this time an octave higher and a decibel louder.

"I don't know."

Connie and I stepped outside the van, hoping a plan would come to us as we opened the back of the van and searched for the spare tire.

A man walked toward us. He seemed oblivious to the rain. "Where'd he come from?" Connie asked in a hushed voice.

"I don't know." For miles, we hadn't seen car headlights in front of us or behind us. Our van was the only vehicle on the side of the road.

"Can I help you?" the man asked when he came close.

I can't explain it, but something about his pleasant voice, and perhaps the way he walked, made me feel safe. He wore a white T shirt and was probably in his late twenties.

"We need help," I said. "We have a flat tire–"

"But we don't know where the spare tire is," Connie said.

"That's okay. I'm familiar with this van." He smiled and said, "Don't worry. I know where things are, and I can take care of it."

I thought it strange that he would know about this van, especially since it was new, but I didn't argue.

Despite the rain, he changed the tire and put the flat one in the back of the van. "Is there anything else I can do for you?" he asked.

"No, we're fine now." Connie opened the driver's side door, scrambled to find her purse, and pulled out a twenty-dollar bill. "Thank you so much for your help." She held out the money.

"That's all right. Glad to do it."

Connie insisted, but he shook his head. "If there's nothing else I can do, and you're sure you're okay, I'll be on my way." He waved and walked back the way he had come, from behind our van.

We yelled good-bye and thanked him several more times. Then I could no longer see him. "He seems to have disappeared as quickly as he appeared," I said.

"He can't just walk in this horrible rain," Connie said. "But I didn't see any headlights or taillights."

"I didn't hear a door open or close," I said.

Where did he go? Did that really just happen? Who was he?

Just then I thought about our girls. We hadn't heard a word from them. "Do you think they're scared?" I whispered.

"I don't know," Connie said. "And how can we possibly explain to them what to us is unexplainable?"

Connie and I slid into the van, and tried to control the shivers from our soaked clothes. We turned to face our daughters.

"Amanda? Darcy?" I asked, "Are you two doing okay?"

The girls sat quietly in the back. They were surprisingly calm.

"Yes, Mom." Amanda's voice sounded peaceful. "We're fine."

"Did you see what happened?" Connie said. "A man came out of nowhere and–"

"Amanda and I were freaking out when the van started shaking," Darcy said, "and when the thunder crashed–"

"That made it even worse," Amanda said, "and I was afraid."

"Amanda said we should pray and God would take care of us. That's what we did."

Connie and I had been so caught up in what was going on that we hadn't thought to pray.

"We prayed that God would keep us safe," Amanda said.

"We needed help, so we asked God to send someone," Darcy said. "God sent that nice man."

"We knew God would take care of us."

"God sent an angel to help us," Darcy said.

Connie and I marveled at the innocent faith of our young daughters. As we drove along, I kept rethinking that event, and spontaneously thanked God for caring and taking care of us, even though I hadn't asked.

That August night, we learned an important lesson. As Christians, we knew God was with us, but until that incident I didn't realize how easily the Lord answers our prayers. As we drove home, I kept thinking of a verse I had known for years, but now it took on relevance: "Don't worry about anything; instead pray about everything. Tell God what you need and thank him for all he has done" (Philippians 4:6).

Our daughters grasped the lesson before we did.

As we understood later, it took an angel to convince us.

CHAPTER THREE

Heavenly Trio

Don Piper

Most people who know me know I died on January 18, 1989, went to heaven, and was prayed back to earth about ninety minutes later; however, many don't know the rest of the story—a part I didn't know until more than a year afterward.

One powerful element came out when I ate at a Chinese restaurant with Dick and Anita Onerecker. We had just come from church, where Dick served as the senior pastor. They had invited me to preach.

My first encounter with Dick and Anita had been in the piney woods of East Texas. They were part of a leadership team for a church growth conference that ended on a Wednesday.

On a cold, rain-slicked rural road a few miles from the gates of the retreat center, a tractor-trailer truck crossed the center stripe of the two-lane highway on a bridge over Lake Livingston, and hit me head-on. I was killed instantly.

The report stated, "Dead on the scene," and they summoned the coroner. Although the accident involved three cars, there were no serious injuries to the other people.

Because of the accident, traffic backed up in both directions. Dick and Anita also headed home from the conference. They had stopped for take-out coffee, and were half-a-mile from the accident. With so many cars backed up, they left their car and walked to the scene of the accident to see if they could be of assistance.

Anita gave her hot coffee to an elderly man in one of the other accident vehicles. Dick sought out the emergency medical technicians.

After Dick identified himself, one EMT said, "The man in the red car is dead; several people are badly shaken up, but not seriously hurt."

Weeks after the accident, Dick told me, "The Lord spoke to me in a clear voice:

'Pray for the man in the red car.'"

When Dick asked permission to get under the tarp that now covered my red Escort, an EMT refused. "The demolished car is too gruesome."

Dick persisted and the man relented. Despite the misty rain, Dick pulled back the tarp and crawled inside my Escort. He found my horribly mangled body slumped in the front seat. He prayed desperately for me, not knowing at that time for whom he was praying.

Even my intimate friends would not have recognized me. Both legs were crushed, one was severed. So was my left arm. My chest was impaled by the steering wheel. In addition to obvious wounds, I was bleeding from the ears and eyes.

My best recollection of what I heard, and the one I related to Dick's church, was that Dick had taken hold of my only intact limb, my right hand, and prayed fervently and urgently. He prayed that I would live and be delivered from internal injuries. He paused a few times and sang hymns. At one point he began singing, "What a Friend We Have in Jesus."

I started to sing with Dick.

At the shock of hearing my singing with him, he scurried from under the tarp and yelled, "The man is alive!"

Once again, he crawled under the tarp and continued to pray—with even more intensity. We continued to sing while firefighters, now on the scene, tried to extricate me.

I was unaware of the activity, so I can only report what Dick and others told me. I had been driving along Texas Highway 19 on my way to lead a Wednesday prayer service at our church in Alvin, a suburb of Houston. On the bridge above Lake Livingston, a huge truck came at me.

In my next moment of consciousness I was in the darkness, singing hymns along with a voice I didn't recognize. The powerful hand that gripped mine infused me with strength, encouragement, and the will to survive.

More than a year passed after my ordeal, and most of that time I was in a hospital bed and underwent sixteen surgeries (more would follow). Excruciating pain filled my body constantly.

Because of God's grace I slowly recovered and within a year I was able to preach at Dick's church. I wore heavy leg braces and was still in agony, but I was alive and able to stand at the pulpit of the man who had prayed me back to life.

I told Dick's congregation about their pastor's fervent prayers, our hymn singing in the wrecked car, and his strong hand that supported me and infused me with courage to hold on.

Many people cried that day–and tears came to my own eyes as I relived that experience.

✦ ✦ ✦ ✦ ✦

While we ate lunch after the worship service, Anita smiled and leaned toward me. "I need to correct something you said in the pulpit this morning."

I returned her smile but I thought, *that's exactly what every preacher doesn't want to hear.*

"I enjoyed hearing your testimony this morning. I know it wasn't easy for you–"

"No, it wasn't–"

"There's just one thing. The part where you talked about Dick holding your hand and praying for you–"

I nodded.

"That didn't happen."

"I have many gaps in my memory, Anita, and some of my facts come from those who were there. But of one thing I am absolutely positive. I vividly remember holding his hand. That's what inspired me to hold on. I remember–"

"You *were* holding a hand as Dick prayed." She peered intently at me. "But it wasn't Dick's hand."

I don't know if I protested or stared silently. "But how–"

"No one could have reached your hand while you were trapped inside your car. You were twisted so far to the right that your right hand was actually on the floor of the passenger's side."

She paused and I nodded.

"Dick reached through the back window of your car."

"That's correct and–"

"Dick placed his right arm between the front seats and your right shoulder–your unbroken arm."

"That's right–"

"Your right hand was beyond Dick's reach."

I stared at her uncomprehendingly. "But I remember the hand–it was so powerful. I *know* a hand grasped mine. I drew enormous strength and help from that hand. It gave me the power to hang on."

"There was a hand all right." She paused and added, "But it wasn't Dick's."

"If it wasn't Dick's hand, whose hand was it?"

"I believe you know."

Just then I understood. God sent one of His ministering spirits—an angel—not only to hold my hand but also to infuse me with a will to live.

There had been three of us inside that demolished car. It had been a heavenly trio.

CHAPTER FOUR

The Climb and the Crevasse

Roy Peterson and Wes Peterson

Roy:

I wanted a special birthday present for my son Jordan's tenth birthday. In 1990, we lived in Quito, Ecuador, where I worked for Wycliffe Bible Translators so we couldn't just give him a typical American party.

I got the idea of making Jordan's birthday a father-son hike on the volcano Cotopaxi. On September 10, I took Jordan, my twelve-year-old son Wes, and twenty others. We loaded up two vans to explore the mountain.

Cotopaxi is one of the highest, most active volcanoes in the world and has erupted more than fifty times since 1738. On many days, we couldn't see the top of the volcano because of heavy clouds. Yet it's a beautiful sight, and I wanted it to be an experience Jordan and the others wouldn't forget.

After a two-hour drive, we began our hike at ten thousand feet. It was a nice climb, and we had no thoughts of reaching the summit because the area is ice-covered all year. Besides that, we would have needed special gear, such as ice picks and crampons on our shoes.

By lunch we had made it to the Jose Ribas Refuge at 15,740 feet, which had a primitive wooden structure to protect climbers from wind. The ice-and-glacier line was only a short distance farther up the mountain; the boys and fathers were having so much fun we didn't want to stop.

After several more minutes of hiking, we crossed the line from dirt to ice glacier. We were naturally excited by our accomplishment. We weren't able to see the crevasses on the glacier. Crevasses are usually nearly vertical and are especially treacherous when a light coating of snow or ice covers their surface. The weight of unsuspecting climbers breaks the crust, and they plunge to their deaths.

✦ ✦ ✦ ✦ ✦

Wes:

We had fun climbing the mountain. We reached an amazing spot where the trails turned from dirt into ice. We probably should have stopped and gone back down. Instead, we climbed or jumped over obstacles in the pathway.

If we had been dressed for the ice, I suppose it might have been all right, but we wore only sneakers and light winter coats. At sixteen thousand feet we reached a place with a tremendous amount of ice. Although I was only twelve years old, my sense was that we stared at something the size of two football fields of nothing but flat, solid ice. It was one of the most awe-inspiring places I'd ever seen and the highest on a mountain I'd ever climbed.

That was too much fun for us to miss. Without asking, we ran out onto the massive sheets of ice. We slid, pushed, and played as only kids can do in a newfound wonderland. I wanted to keep exploring and ventured away from the group. Without my realizing it, the ice angled down the mountain and I began to slide. Sliding faster and faster, it was getting harder to stay on my feet.

Just then I realized I was heading toward a crevasse. I couldn't stop and I couldn't avoid it. I glimpsed into the crevasse, and sunlight disappeared into darkness. I believed those were my last moments. My body slid toward the crevasse with my friends behind me, endless white ice in front of me, a massive mountain to my right, and on my left a crevasse the width of my view. I was so close.

With my left foot inches from the crevasse, a recognizable sound of metal clanging and grinding into ice filled my ears. Before I could look around, two large arms wrapped around my body and lifted me off the ice. He pulled me close to his chest and turned toward the mountain and my friends.

They watched as he effortlessly carried me thirty feet back to where they stood. He didn't say a word. Dad saw us coming and hurried toward us. As soon as we reached the others, my rescuer put me on the ground. I stood there, shocked and amazed. The group gathered around me.

"Are you all right?" Dad asked as he knelt in front of me and hugged me. "Were you trying to scare us?"

"What happened?" someone asked.

"I was having fun sliding, but then I couldn't stop. No matter what I did, I kept slipping down. About one second before I reached that deep crevasse–" I pointed to it. "A man came and saved me."

"Where is he?" Dad asked. We all looked out onto the bright sheets of ice to thank the person.

"I don't know." I looked around and couldn't see him. "He was standing right behind me when he put me down." Except for the huddled group, we were alone with nothing but white space everywhere.

"He's gone!" Dad yelled. "I saw him! I saw him carrying Wes!"

"I didn't see his face because he was wearing a ski mask and goggles." I took a deep breath and said, "And he was decked out in full hiking gear."

"Were you scared?" one of my friends asked.

I shook my head no, and it wasn't that I was trying to appear brave. Once those arms wrapped around me I was filled with peace, and all fear was gone.

"But where is he?" another father asked.

"He couldn't be gone this quickly," a third father said.

None of us had spoken to him, and the man didn't say a word to me. Dad had watched him carry me and put me down. We weren't in a place where someone could just turn a bend and disappear. It would have taken quite a while, at least five minutes, before anyone could have walked out of the line of sight in any direction.

CHAPTER FIVE

Stranger at the Door

William E. Reece with Colleen L. Reece

I'd never seen a winter storm that bad before. We lived in Northwest Washington. Just before Christmas, snow had started in the early afternoon and blanketed everything. I shivered as I made my way from the barn into the house. I stepped into the warm kitchen. A blast of icy air fluttered the curtains, making the flames in the kerosene lamps flicker.

"Shut the door!" my little sister Lucy yelled. "We have to keep baby Jim warm."

I slammed the door, got out of my snow-laden coat, and hung it on a hook, with a pan beneath to catch the drips. "I hoped he would be better," I said.

Tears leaped to Lucy's worried brown eyes. "At least he's sleeping."

"I thought for sure the medicine the doctor brought earlier today would break his fever," my second sister Alza said.

That morning the doctor had poured medicine into a bottle. "Keep him warm and give him this every four hours. The fever should run its course in a few days."

He had done all he could for my baby brother and had other patients to attend to. After the first dose, Jim went to sleep.

When we stared out the windows and listened to the howling winds, we knew the storm had turned into a full-scale blizzard. Ma and the girls prepared supper. Pa blessed the food. In the middle of his prayer, baby Jim coughed.

Ma hurried to the hand-carved cradle in the corner and put her lips to Jim's forehead. "He's burning up."

"The medicine should have done something by now," I said. "Do you want me to go get the doctor?" It was five miles to his house. There would be heavy drifts and the snow was already several inches deep. But I was the oldest son and felt I should go.

Ma shook her head. "You'll never get through the drifts. Neither would the doctor and his buggy."

"He can't do anything else," Pa said. "He's done what he could."

"I'll try to cool Jim by sponging him off," Ma said and told us to eat our supper.

"Ma's a good nurse," Pa said quietly. His words seemed to reassure the girls, my younger brother Bob, and me. After we silently finished our meal, Alza and Lucy cleared the table and washed the dishes. The fireplace roared and flames heat up the room, burning great lengths of logs I'd helped fell and split. Bob and I sat on the wood floor and mended a harness.

Time passed and no one spoke. Worry about baby Jim left us with nothing to say. The ferocious wail of the wind occasionally broke the silence.

Just then, a loud knock jarred all of us.

"What's that?" I asked, but no one seemed to know. "It couldn't be anybody out there in this blizzard." I turned back to the harness.

The thump was louder the second time.

"Someone is at the door!" I jumped up to answer.

A man stood on the porch.

"Come in!" I motioned the snow-clad figure to come into the room and shut out the storm. "Warm yourself. I'll see to your horse."

"I have no horse," he said in a quiet voice. "Would you have something I could eat?"

"No horse?" I asked. "How could you–"

"Don't keep the poor man standing in his wet coat," Ma called out. "Girls, give our visitor something to eat."

Lucy and Alza filled a plate with the remains of supper. The cornbread was still warm and we had a lot of beans and pickle relish. Alza poured him a glass of milk.

"I'm sorry it isn't more," Lucy said as she set it on the table before the stranger. "It's all we have left."

"This will be fine." He took off his coat. Without saying anything else, he began to eat. I kept peeking at him, wondering how he could get to our isolated farmhouse in a storm like this. The roads didn't even look like roads. How did he find us? Was he lost? I started to ask him, but just then Jim screamed.

"He's sick," Alza said to the stranger, "but Ma's a good nurse."

"Don't worry," the stranger said and smiled. "The baby will be fine." He went on eating. After he finished, he stood and put on his coat.

"You can't go out there," Pa said. "You'll get lost or freeze—"

"Thank you for the food. I'll be going now," he said and walked out the door.

"Run after him!" Pa yelled to me. "He can stay with us tonight."

I ran to the door and opened it. "Come back!" I shouted. Between the snow and the wind I couldn't see anything. "We have room for you, Mister! Come back!"

He didn't answer.

"Bring him back," Pa said.

I grabbed my coat. "Light a lantern," I told Bob.

Not more than a full minute passed before I stepped outside the door. Almost immediately, I opened it again. "Come here, Pa."

Pa came out. Bob and the girls crowded behind him. Lantern light mingled with the light from the room and shone on the porch, steps, and front yard. I pointed to the heavy layer of snow. "Look."

"Not a footprint," Pa said and we heard the shock in his voice.

"Where'd he go?" Bob asked.

Pa, Bob, and I stood on the porch. Pa took the lantern and held it high. He walked from one end of the porch to the other and kept shaking his head. "Snow couldn't have covered his prints that quickly."

Bob and I tried to see some sign of him. We never did.

We finally went back inside. None of us could explain his disappearance. "We all saw him," Bob said. "So how could he vanish like that?"

"He ate from that plate," Alza said and pointed.

Just then Lucy yelled, "Ma says come quickly. Jim's better!"

"His fever broke," she said and smiled. "Jim is sleeping peacefully."

"Praise the Mighty Lord!" Pa said.

"The stranger–the stranger said Jim would be fine," I said. "How did he know? Who was he?"

Pa's blue eyes looked into mine. He reached for the well-used family Bible and opened it to Hebrews 13:2 (KJV). "Be not forgetful to entertain strangers: for thereby some have entertained angels unawares," he read.

"Was the stranger *an angel*?" Lucy asked.

Pa closed his well-worn Bible. "I don't know. I *do* know that no human being can walk in the snow without leaving tracks."

Some people try to explain that story to tell us it wasn't a miracle. We don't care what others say. For us it was a miracle–to remind us that God still cared about us and our needs, even if He had to send an angel to make it happen.

CHAPTER SIX

Angel on the Shoulder

Ellen Cardwell

D on and I were on our honeymoon, driving down California's Highway 1. Rugged cliffs rose to the left, ocean waves splashed close by my side. Friends insisted we borrow their car—it was their contribution to our wedding. The cars we owned were reliable enough for driving around town, but not for a road trip.

We left Highland's Inn at Carmel-by-the-Sea, where we had spent our first three days as a married couple.

We headed south toward Hearst Castle, recently opened for sightseeing tours. At that time there was little, if anything, human-made between Carmel and our destination. It was as if civilization hadn't reached that far, and we were alone at the edge of the continent. The beauty of God's creation completely engulfed us. We absorbed the peaceful scenery into our dry souls like sponges, drained by the preparations and celebrations of previous days.

We rode along in refreshing silence until the car started acting strangely. *What's the matter?* I wondered out loud, suddenly feeling apprehensive.

Don pulled the vehicle over to the narrow shoulder and admitted, "I don't know." Neither one of us knew much about cars. We'd passed no gas stations, nor was there one as far as the eye could see. And cell phones hadn't been invented. We were totally helpless. *What now?*

Just then, a man emerged from a door in the hillside opposite us and he stepped onto a wooden landing. We hadn't noticed a door until then. It was flush with the mountainside, midway between the top and bottom. He walked down a long flight of railed stairs that hugged the rocky scenery. He looked rather ordinary and not particularly handsome. He was maybe forty years old, and he was dressed in work clothes. He came up to the driver's side window. I was relieved to see kindness in his eyes.

"What's the problem?"

"I don't have any idea," my husband admitted.

"I have a car just like this one. Do you mind if I take a look? I have an idea what the problem might be."

"Not at all. Please do."

The kind stranger showed Don what knob to pull, then walked around in front. We watched, stunned, as he lifted the hood, poked around underneath, and popped his head back up after only moments.

"I think you'll be all right now," he reassured us, wiping his hands. Before we could ask what the problem was or find out how much he charged, he was headed across the road, disappearing the same way he came.

We looked at each other, not knowing what to make of it. We hadn't even thanked him. All we could do was thank our heavenly Father repeatedly for sending us the help we needed. In today's vernacular we would say it was a God-thing.

Many years have intervened since then, and now, because we know more, we believe the stranger was an angel on the shoulder of the road. He had no wings, nor was he wearing a flowing white robe. Instead, he was quick to respond, humble in manner, with the know-how and ability to solve the problem and freely serving us without expecting anything in return. Aren't those heavenly qualities?

More lasting than the benefit of his appearance is the message he brought us. From then on we knew we weren't alone. Even when we're without the help of friends, pastors, or natural resources, God is always with us, caring for us. Our heavenly Father was "there" for us then, is "here" for us now, and will be as long as we live.

CHAPTER SEVEN

A Hospital Angel

Margee Dyck

Our home hadn't been a peaceful place in recent months because we sensed the tension between our parents. Our security had been shaken by the uncertainty of the future. We whispered frightening words like "separation" and "divorce" to each other in the darkness of our bedroom.

As a ten-year-old girl, I often lay awake until the early morning hours, wondering what the future held and if God was watching over our family.

One stifling summer evening, our family tried to escape the heat by going outside to benefit from the coolness of the front yard. My siblings and I flopped on the grass to enjoy rare moments of serenity and happiness.

That night on the grass felt almost like old times with laughter and closeness. Our father, lying on his back, gave us "airplane rides." One at a time, each of us sat on his feet. He'd spin us around, send us flying into the air, and we'd land on the soft grass. We pushed and shoved to get our share of turns, enjoying the thrill of the ride and the attention of our father who had been distant in recent months.

When my turn came again, I squealed in excitement as my father gave me an unusually hard push. Instead of going straight ahead, however, I twisted sideways and landed awkwardly on my left arm. A loud snap told us it was broken. I felt excruciating pain, and listened to my mother's concern and my father's remorse.

After hurried arrangements for caregivers for my siblings, my father put me in the car. My mother used a pillow to support my arm.

My parents took me to a small, neighborhood clinic. A technician took an X-ray that showed a complicated two-bone break, so they kept me overnight. They had no doctor available, but a nurse told me, "We'll put a cast on in the morning."

My parents, assured I would be all right, said goodnight and left me in the care of the two nurses.

My memories of that terrible night still remain hazy. My arm was more painful than anything I had ever experienced, and my whole body seemed to ache in sympathy. A nurse put me into a hard, cold hospital bed and closed the door.

I was alone, in pain, and felt overwhelmed with fear and loneliness. I must have dozed off because I wakened after what seemed like a brief, exhausted sleep. I was chilled and felt unbelievable throbbing and torture. The cold worsened and I shivered violently because of the ice they had packed around my arm. Crying, I called out repeatedly, hoping one of the nurses would hear me.

No one came.

My parents had taught me that God is always with us, so I finally prayed and begged God to warm me up and take away the pain.

Just then, the room grew bright. Warmth and peace swept over me as a beautiful nurse with golden hair and a radiant smile stood next to my bed. "My name is Gloria," she said. She sang softly as she fitted a warmed blanket around me. I drifted into a tranquil sleep and slept deeply for the rest of the night.

The next morning my parents returned, the doctor set my arm, and put on a cast. Before we left the clinic, I told my mother about Gloria and her kindness to me during the night. "I want to go the nurses' station," I said, "and thank the wonderful nurse for caring for me."

Although Mother was in a hurry, I persisted, so she agreed. We went back down the hall to the nurses' station to find Gloria. I looked around and didn't see her anywhere, so we walked over to talk to the nurse on duty.

"My daughter refuses to leave without saying thank you to the nurse who came into her room last night with a warmed blanket and sang to her."

"Can you tell her how much I appreciated what she did?" I asked.

"Of course," she said.

The nurse smiled as I recounted Gloria's kindness and told her how much I appreciated her because I was scared and hurt badly. Confusion spread over the nurse's face. "There were only two nurses on duty last night," she said after I finished, "and neither is named Gloria."

"You know the one I mean," I said. "She was the slim one with the blonde hair."

"I know all the nurses at this clinic," the woman said. "We have absolutely no one with that name."

"But she came into my room and—"

"Besides, both of the nurses on duty last night are brunettes."

The nurse and my mother looked at each other and chuckled. "She must have dreamed it," my mother said.

I didn't argue, but I knew the truth. Gloria was real and the warm blanket was real. I knew what happened: God had sent an angel to comfort a scared, lonely, ten-year-old little girl during that long night.

I knew something else: Because God cared about me, everything was going to be all right. By sending Gloria when I was in such pain, God showed He would continue to watch over me throughout my life, no matter what happened in the future.

My parents worked out their difficulties, stayed together, and our family became happy once again. I grew up assured that God is interested in all the details of our lives, our troubles, fears, and hurts.

I knew then—and still believe today—that when His children cry out in need, God hears.

Sometimes He sends one of His own special messengers to meet their needs.

CHAPTER EIGHT

Alligator Alley Angels

DiAne Gates

Mother called it my gypsy lifestyle; I called it the dream of a lifetime. Earlier that spring I left a *normal* job and joined the freelance art market, traveling to weekend art shows throughout the Southeast to sell my work.

The spring and summer shows felt like weekends at Disneyland. Then I had an opportunity to travel to Marco Island, Florida, for a significant trade show. My husband couldn't go and our children were in school. I didn't want to drive alone, so my friend Darlene joyfully agreed to go with me.

Our husbands agreed to keep the children, and we left Orlando on a Thursday afternoon, headed for a girls' time out and a successful show for me.

We planned to drive to Naples, spend the night with Darlene's brother, and continue to Marco Island the next day. We crammed my '64 Rambler station wagon to capacity and took off. We laughed and sang. Free-spirits, having the time of our lives.

Until dark.

The last town before Naples had long lines at the gas station. Already running late, I figured we could make it to Naples or, if not, we'd surely find another gas station along the way.

A few miles down the road a large sign appeared in the beam of our headlights: Toll Road. Shortcut to Naples. Alligator Alley. The last four words stood out: No gas 30 miles.

My gas gauge didn't work, but I knew my car and I was sure we could make the next thirty miles. So we started down Alligator Alley.

The two-lane road crossed the Florida peninsula from Miami to Naples and crossed through the middle of the everglades. Sunset over the glades lifted the curtain to another world that sprang to life and I imagined creeping, slithery things with large teeth, nocturnal eyes, and terrifying calls in the night.

We finally tired of singing. Darlene dug the cigarettes from her purse and lit up. The end of her cigarette, headlights on our car, and the occasional car that met us were the only relief from the unrelenting blackness.

We drove in silence, lulled by the hum of the motor and Darlene's rhythmic puffs. Just then the car choked and sputtered.

"Uh-oh," I said. "We should have stopped for gas."

The engine died. I guided the vehicle to a stop on the narrow shoulder of the road.

"We're out of gas!" Darlene screamed. "Dick's going to kill you. If we live to get out of this mess."

"Hey, you were in on the vote not to wait in line for gas."

"I know. But what are we going to do now?" She bit her lip before she said, "We can't just sit here."

"We've got to be calm. Someone will stop and help." I wasn't sure I believed the words I said to her.

"We can't sit here." Darlene ground her cigarette out on the sole of her shoe and flung the car door open. "I'm getting out of the car to see what's out there."

I grabbed her arm. "You can't do that. A snake might bite you or you could be attacked by a bear or gator. Stay put. Someone will see us and stop."

I had hardly spoken before a beat-up El Camino pulled to a stop in front of us. Two grungy-looking men wearing muscle shirts, with do-rags holding back their stringy hair, got out and approached the car.

We were two women alone on a dark, deserted road. Their presence filled me with fear, and I fought terror as they came closer.

The doors didn't lock–and I hoped they wouldn't try them. Darlene grabbed a hammer from my toolbox inside the car. I pulled out my roadside emergency flashlight. I rolled down the window an inch, lowered my voice an octave, and shined the blinding beam in their faces. "At the tollbooth, will you report that we have car trouble?" I asked.

"Sure," one of them said. "Anything else we can do?"

"Just that."

They turned to walk back to their car, then suddenly wheeled around and walked back toward us.

"Dear Lord, please protect us," I cried softly.

Again I aimed the beam of the flashlight onto their faces. One of them called back, "Turn your lights on when a car approaches, then off when they pass so your battery won't go dead."

"I'll do that!"

They left.

We breathed a sigh of relief. Until we remembered—*we were once again alone in the darkness.*

I gazed into the heavens, asked forgiveness for every wrong thing I'd ever done, and promised God if He delivered us I wouldn't be so stupid again.

For the next hour we listened to unidentifiable sounds in the night, waiting for help to come. We were able to see only the flare of Darlene's match as she whittled down her once-full package of artificial comfort.

I was scared.

Just then, car lights sprang across the horizon. Dots at first, growing larger along with my sense of both hope and fear. Darlene was so excited she started to get out of the car and wave them down.

"I'm going to get them," Darlene said.

"Who knows what they're doing out here?"

We waited. Darlene smoked. I prayed. The car drove back out of the swamp, turned toward us, and slowed. As the vehicle came even with us, the driver lowered his window a notch to reveal a well-dressed man and woman.

"Do you need help?" he asked.

Darlene screamed, "Yes! Yes!" She leaped from the car and shouted at me, "Get out of the car so they can see we're helpless!"

I hesitated but followed her instructions. The man pulled over, got out, and checked under the hood. After confirming that the car was out of gas, he said, "It's dangerous out here."

"It wasn't our intention to be stranded out here," I said, and Darlene explained what had happened.

He handed me his business card. "I have a paving business in town and have gas at the warehouse," he said. "Come with us. We'll get the gas, bring you back, and get you on your way."

Darlene said, "There's a woman with him so I'm sure it's all right." She jumped into the backseat of their car before I could think.

"What about my artwork?" I asked, but Darlene was already in her side of the car. I had to leave everything in my unlocked car in the middle of the darkness. The only other choice was staying with the stuff—by myself. I jumped inside the car and prayed all the way while the man drove.

He took us to a warehouse. A gas pump was right in front of the building, so I relaxed. While the man filled a can, the woman took us into the office. "Why don't you phone your husbands so they don't worry?"

We thanked her and made the calls. Then the couple drove us back to the car. He poured the gas into the tank and made sure the car started. After it did, they followed us to the outskirts of Naples.

We arrived at Darlene's brother's house an hour later and called our husbands to let them know we were safe. My husband Dick listened before quietly asking for the name and number of our rescuers so he could call to thank them. I read off the number from the business card.

The next morning we set up my display at the Marco Island show next to a local participant. He heard our story and said, "I'd never be out on Alligator Alley at night. When I go out there in the daytime I carry a shotgun and an extra can of gas. Four-legged creatures aren't the only danger in that wilderness."

I smiled and thought, *I'm glad I didn't know how dangerous it was.* I had been frightened enough as it was.

The show was a huge success, and we phoned our husbands to let them know we were headed home.

"Oh, one other thing," Dick said. "You know the man's phone number you gave me from his card?" He asked me to repeat it and I did.

"That's it, all right. I called. There's no such number. No business by that name and no such address."

"We were there last night. We walked into the warehouse and called you from that same number. You must have dialed it wrong."

"I've tried several times," Dick said, "and it always comes up as a wrong number."

The following week I made numerous calls to the number on the card, but I received the same information my husband did. I couldn't locate anyone or anything to confirm that the man and woman existed, or that such a number or business by that name operated in Florida.

✦ ✦ ✦ ✦ ✦

Were they angels? I don't know. But I do know this—God snatched two foolish young women from the jaws of danger and darkness that night and gave us renewed life.

With God's help I'm attempting to live in light of the promise I made in the depth of that despair—*never to be that stupid again*. But I still smile when I think of this story. Even in my naïveté, God took care of me.

CHAPTER NINE

A Lost Little Bear

Pamela Dowd

At LaGuardia Airport in New York City, one chilly November morning, Abigail hugged her ragged teddy bear good-bye one final time. She carefully hid him under shoes in her purple backpack.

"Shouldn't I carry my backpack on the plane like always?" she asked. "You sure he'll be safe riding under the plane, Mom?"

Considering we had three terminals to hike through before arriving home, I reassured her from my years of traveling ease, "Tah-Bear will be fine. Don't worry."

For twelve years Abigail had carried her tattered teddy on every family vacation. With his crumpled red felt tie, faded business attire, and a broken eye resembling a wide-eyed wink, he was *hers*, not something she could readily claim for many other items in her twin-shared world.

Hours later, we stood in an almost vacant regional airport staring at an empty conveyor belt. Seven of the eight bags we'd checked had arrived, and we stacked them at our feet.

Abigail's purple backpack hadn't. I told my husband, "She wouldn't have sent him inside her backpack this morning if I hadn't insisted he'd fly safe by himself."

Abigail's eyes glistened with tears. I hugged my girl tightly. "Surely it'll come soon." *Lord, make it appear.*

The sliding metal carousel door slammed shut. I leaned over the conveyor and banged on the door. My knuckles rapped like pelting hail.

A slender, young baggage handler poked his dark head around the cargo area door. "Yes? You missing a bag?"

"We're missing a *bear*. It's *inside* a bag. It's purple, not the bear, the backpack." I wasn't sure how much sense I was making, but I was frantic. "Surely it's here. Maybe on your cart or maybe in the plane. Could you check? It's small and easily overlooked."

He stared at me as if I spoke a foreign language. I willed myself to calmness, but despair seeped in. A bear so loved couldn't just disappear.

"Step around to the counter, please. I'll meet you there." The door swung shut.

Our three daughters trailed me like ducklings while Dad went to retrieve the car. The normal missing baggage claim desk had closed for the night. My husband, the realist, wasn't fretting. That's because he didn't share my dire imaginings—anyone could walk away with a backpack in 1995.

The baggage handler tried to engage me in lighthearted conversation about local tourist events as he struggled to type my information. I had to repeat everything twice, three times, and spell out each answer.

As I looked around I realized he was the sole employee in the empty terminal—the one person who was trying to find Tah-Bear. His slow, hunt-and-peck method edged me toward total loss of control.

Be patient, he's doing someone else's job.

He told me he'd never heard of a route and box number for an address. How could he not recognize the town I live in, a mere sixty miles away? I envisioned myself swinging his computer monitor around, grabbing the keyboard, and taking charge. Instead, I forced a smile and waited.

The printer finally whined and produced a dot matrix printout. He tore the detachable edges and folded the sheet in half. His attention to detail *was* admirable. "Only one more thing." He poked around until he produced a small pamphlet. "This tells you standard airline procedure." He stapled it to the printout. "I'm sorry about your bag."

I reached for the paperwork, sorely regretful for my negativity and impatience. "Thank you for all your help."

Abigail didn't complain with I-told-you-so assertions on the ride home. I almost wished she had—then my misery could overflow and the tears I held back could stream out of me.

Every few minutes my husband offered comforting statements such as, "He'll show up" and "Don't worry."

His words didn't help me, but I said little. The other two girls didn't say so, but I could tell they were glad their bears were safe at home.

We got all three children to bed at 2:30 AM. Abigail hugged me tight, in spite of my culpability. "Don't worry, Mama. God will bring Tah-Bear home."

"Yes, darling, I'm sure He will," I said, but I doubted the truthfulness of my words.

I awakened at six o'clock, and the instant recall of a few hours earlier spun through my mind. *Is nothing sacred anymore? God, help me. You can see Abigail's backpack, wherever it is. Nothing in all of creation is hidden from Your sight. Please help Tah-Bear come home.*

At 8:00 AM, I dialed the airline and told our mournful story to an agent who immediately understood. "My nine-year-old won't go anywhere without her favorite doll either." Empathy led her to initiate searches through the three terminals we had jet-sped across. She promised to do everything she could to help us.

Enthused, I returned to bed. *Lord, work even this out for good. Thank You that Abigail isn't agonizing over the loss of her most cherished earthly possession.* "Hold everything loosely," I told myself.

At noon I discovered that the missing bag's number nowhere resembled the others' sequential order. *That's strange—we checked all our bags at the same time.* I called the airline and described the

LaGuardia skycap's hasty demeanor and my discovery of the oddly numbered claim tags.

This time, sympathy came from a young woman who still traveled with her Pooh Bear. I described Tah-Bear's nubby fur, his fractured eye, tattered black pinstripe business suit, and crumpled red tie. I heard her fingers tap, tap, flying over the keyboard. Capable comfort.

For what seemed like half an hour, while she kept me on the line, the woman processed ground checks and followed up on every imaginable lead. Before she hung up, she promised to keep checking. I didn't give up. Each time I called, a new clerk read my file and made my call a pleasant experience.

Abigail was often by my side, and as we prayed together I witnessed her simple, childlike faith and fearless courage. She never wavered in believing Tah-Bear would arrive home safely.

I wasn't so sure.

The ringing telephone roused me at two o'clock the following morning. A man with a poor cell connection requested directions to our home. I finally figured out who he was, so my husband and I went to the front door to await the courier.

At 3:00 AM, twenty-six hours after we declared Tah-Bear missing, a man dressed in a fedora, overcoat, suit, and red tie arrived at our front door. An airline representative? I was confused by his appearance. I peeked over my husband's shoulder and whispered, "How did he get through the community security gate without calling us first to open it for him?"

His large black Cadillac idled in the cold morning, producing frosted exhaust clouds behind him. He didn't appear to be an airport official or airline employee. Indeed, he looked a little like Tah-Bear had before love tattered Tah's clothes and fur.

The man bowed politely, smiled like a saint, and handed my husband the purple backpack. I grabbed it from my husband and hurried upstairs. I opened it and found Abigail's Tah-Bear. After I tucked the bear into Abigail's arms, tears ran down my cheeks at God's grace in caring for the need of my daughter.

Abigail gave me a drowsy smile and hugged Tah-Bear tightly. As I walked back to bed I thought of the elegantly dressed stranger with the attractive smile and gentle voice.

An angel? Perhaps. An answer to prayer? Definitely.

I still don't know how he got through security–and neither do the security people. So far as I know, the airline never did locate the missing bag. But that doesn't matter.

What does matter is that God cared enough about a 'tween-ager to guide her tattered bear safely home. The Lord cared enough about me to create a valuable lesson: My fret-filled calls hadn't moved heaven; a young girl's resolute faith had.

CHAPTER TEN

Angel in the ICU

Elise Daly Parker

I lay awake and kept telling myself to get up when car wheels squealed to an abrupt halt. I bolted from my bed as I heard people screaming, "Call an ambulance." Stumbling to the phone, I dialed the emergency number. The operator told me help was on the way.

As I made my way downstairs, it occurred to me that I hadn't heard the bus go by, the one my husband Chris took each morning to his office in the city.

Chris would be the first one to run in and call an ambulance, I thought. The bus stop was right on the corner, one house from ours.

As my thoughts raced, so did my heart. I went to my front door. My now panicked voice pierced the warm air and brilliant sunlight of a perfect June day.

"Is it a man?" I yelled to the people surrounding a body lying on the side of the road. Without waiting for an answer, "Does he have a mustache?"

"Yes yes," a serious face turned toward me.

I ran out to the street. A man lay in a fetal position. I couldn't see his face, but I recognized his clothes.

"Chris!" I screamed and raced toward him. I cradled him in my arms. Blood ran from his ears and his eyes were closed. I cried. "I'm here. Hold on, honey. You're going to be okay. Hold on. I need you."

I have no idea how long I held him, but I looked up to see an ambulance and EMTs. One of them gently asked me to move away and I did.

Chris's eyes rolled as if he fought for consciousness.

I left him with the EMTs and raced to my neighbor's house. I asked them to watch my children. When I returned, Chris lay on a gurney and they were lifting him into the ambulance.

"I want to get in. I'm his wife—"

"Sorry, ma'am, but you can't. The situation is too critical."

Although he didn't say so, it seemed obvious to me that they didn't know if Chris would make it to the hospital alive, and they didn't need to try to calm a hysterical wife inside the ambulance.

They rushed off to the nearest state trauma hospital. I followed behind inside a separate emergency vehicle.

"Oh, God, no. Please, God, no." How could this be happening? We were a happy family with three girls, ages two and almost four, and my fourteen-year-old stepdaughter. Chris had a good job that he liked, and I was thrilled to be able to stay home raising our children. My life had seemed so good and normal.

"Oh, God, I'll do anything. Please let my husband be okay." With my hands shaking, I cried as I raced toward the hospital. It took nearly a half hour, and I continued to cry out, "Please let him live."

At the emergency room entrance, several attendants rushed to the aid of the EMTs to get my husband inside the hospital as quickly as possible. I learned later that just as the ambulance pulled in, Chris lost consciousness.

The next several minutes were filled with a flurry of hospital personnel asking me to fill in paperwork. I signed legal waivers so that no one would be held responsible for the outcome of the necessary brain surgery, not even the doctors. They laid out everything that could go wrong, but no one advised or encouraged me.

"Let's just get through this next step," the attending physician said when I begged him to give me hope. "We're going to operate to relieve the pressure on your husband's brain."

"And then what?"

"We'll let you know when he's in recovery."

No matter how many times I asked (and in my anxiety it was often), the answers were the same: "No, we don't know what his condition is now." "Yes, it's true that he might not survive."

I could respond only with a nod and sit quietly and pray. The word had gotten out and our family and friends gathered in the private waiting room. We cried, prayed, and offered words of encouragement to each other.

The morning passed slowly. A doctor or nurse occasionally came into the waiting room. The most information I received was from one nurse, who said, "He's doing all right. The surgery is progressing."

Still no promises. I stopped asking, thankful to know that so far Chris was alive.

"Your husband is out of surgery," a nurse told us. That was the first piece of good news. Chris had survived the surgery. That was all she could tell us.

A doctor stopped in to tell me Chris was in critical but stable condition. He had survived the surgery, but the next few days would tell whether he would live.

A nurse finally led me to the ICU for a five-minute visit. Before I went inside she said, "You're going to see a lot of bandages."

She must have seen the fear in my eyes because she spoke slowly and with a kindness in her voice. "Your husband is in an induced coma to keep him still in the aftermath of the trauma and surgery. Don't be afraid to talk to him. He can probably hear you."

I entered the sterile room, and my husband was unrecognizable because of the swelling, bruised eyes shut tight, and the mummylike bandages wrapped around his head.

"Hi, honey. It's me, Elise."

I touched Chris with trepidation. I didn't want to disturb his battered body.

The monitors beeped. The multiple intravenous lines ran from various bags and bottles that apparently dripped life back into my husband's body by way of the arteries near his heart.

I was able to make the five-minute visits several times. When evening came, the doctor advised all of us to go home. They didn't want us to wear ourselves out. I understood their words, but I didn't want to go so far away. I felt I needed to be close to the hospital.

I stayed with my sister, who lived about half the distance we did from the hospital. I slept for a few hours only because deep exhaustion took hold of my mind and body. I called the nurse in the ICU within seconds of waking. Chris had made it through the night.

I sighed in relief.

Chris was stable, the nurse told me. When I arrived there, he was still in a coma and looked monstrous. They moved him to a private room and I sat at his bedside throughout the day. Chris fidgeted, his legs shifting from side to side. The nurse assured me this was not significant. "It's likely involuntary," she said.

I drank Diet Coke and moved food around on a plate in the hospital cafeteria. Back at the room, I greeted immediate family as Chris' mother, several brothers, and my sisters arrived.

Death was still possible, so all of us knew this could be our last visit with Chris.

"I love you," I said many, many times. Despite my own uncertainty, I added, "You're going to be okay."

I told him what happened, so that when he came out of the coma, the knowledge of his accident would already be planted in his mind.

As the day turned into night, I felt I needed to get home to my girls, yet I was afraid to leave Chris–afraid that he might die in the night. I couldn't do anything for him, but I still felt I needed to be with him as much as possible.

But I had to care for our children. I arrived home to hugs and kisses and one freaked-out teenager. We sat at our dining room table as I ate a little and told the girls that Daddy was away for a short while. I don't recall what I said, but I was thankful that at least two of them were too young to really understand. I felt numb, but strangely at peace.

That night, I fell into bed right after my call to the ICU. Fear greeted me as I closed my eyes, anticipating haunting images, scary flashbacks of my husband, whose bandages made him appear like the walking dead from a horror movie.

Instead, a sense of calm and stillness flowed over my body. Images of my husband were vivid. I was wide awake and yet I could see Chris lying in his bed. The monitors, the bandages, and the IV lines made up part of the picture, but behind Chris was a large figure with a tall, squarish body. I couldn't see the face, but I *knew* it was an angel from God. He stood there and then he wrapped his arms across Chris's chest and hands as if to show me he was protecting Chris. Chris appeared to be at rest, tranquil, even comfortable.

Every night and often during the day, that image flooded my mind for several weeks. Daily I received uncanny peace from the being whose message to me was as if he were saying, "I'm watching over Chris. He's in my hands and he's going to be okay."

When Chris finally awoke, he was confused and disoriented, didn't know who I was at first, couldn't walk or talk sensibly, couldn't feed himself, and lived in a rehabilitation facility for six weeks.

I had an absolute certainty that he would recover. I had what I believed was blessed assurance. And so we pressed on, the figure continuing to appear in my thoughts until my husband returned to our home.

The road to recovery was a long one marked by profound pain yet great triumph.

But the peace, hope, and that tall figure were there until I took Chris home. After that the figure disappeared. He had finished his mission and brought deep peace to a troubled wife.

CHAPTER ELEVEN

Bulgarian Angels

Betty Cornett

After many years in pastoral work in the Southern United States, my husband Tim and I ministered in Eastern Europe. In Sofia, Bulgaria, still a Communist state in 1985, we faced difficult circumstances and encountered obstacles on our journey.

About five hours of driving from our home base in Sofia, we held a week of fruitful and exciting evangelistic meetings.

On the morning of our return, a pastor said, "Snow fell steadily all night." When we asked how much snow, he shrugged as if to say, "The kind that's typical for this time of year." There had already been about two feet of well-packed snow and ice on the ground before we arrived.

When we left, we prayed for God's protection.

Being from Atlanta, where snow is scarce, I was proud that I had learned to maneuver our rented Renault sedan through wintery conditions.

As we traveled, Tim and I rejoiced over the worship services we had enjoyed. We felt good, knowing that the same God Who blessed the people there would be faithful to us in the rest of our ministry.

A few miles into our trip the moderate snowfall changed to a heavy, raging storm. It seemed to happen suddenly.

"Where did this come from?" Tim asked.

"If the storm continues like this," I said, "we'll have a serious problem in returning to Sofia."

Within minutes, the road and fields blended together under several inches of new snow. Tim rubbed his hand against the windshield. I resisted the impulse to tell him it was doing no good. The heater and defroster had stopped working. Our breathing fogged the car windows.

"Looks bad." Until then, Tim had said little, so I knew he was worried. "We need help."

"No one's on this road."

"I noticed."

Fierce winds whipped against the side of the car. The Renault slid, and I struggled to maintain control. My grip on the steering wheel tightened. My arms and body tensed. I tried to relax.

A powerful blast hit the right side of the car and jammed us against an embankment of drifted snow. I tried unsuccessfully to turn the steering wheel. It was impossible to back up, so I shifted gears to rock the car. No matter what I did, nothing worked. We were stuck off the road.

What are we going to do? How long before somebody will find us?

We couldn't survive in subzero temperatures very long, and our gasoline would run out in a couple of hours.

"Lord Jesus, please get us out of this blizzard and safely back to Sofia." I prayed audibly, but nothing happened.

After about thirty minutes, Tim got out and went to the rear of the car to assess how badly we were stuck. He pushed, but our vehicle didn't budge.

He hadn't prepared for this weather and wore only sneakers, three layers of clothing, and no gloves. When he returned, his hands and feet were numbed from the freezing temperature.

"What are we going to do?" I asked. "We're miles from a town, and I haven't seen any houses along the way."

He took a slow, deep breath before he said, "Looks like we're going to have to trust God."

We turned off the engine to conserve fuel, and almost immediately the windows froze. We estimated the outside temperature to be about twenty degrees below zero.

"It seems absurd to just sit here and do nothing," I said. I tried to open my door. It was tight against the snow bank, but I pushed hard and got the door open enough so I could squeeze out.

I stepped into the waist-high snow. "Help us, Lord. It won't be long until the car is completely hidden from any vehicle that passes this way."

I trudged to the rear of the car and cried out, as if I thought God could hear me better outside. "Help us, Jesus! Help us, Jesus!"

Tim left the snow-covered vehicle and stood beside me. I yelled again. "Help us, Jesus! Help us, Jesus!"

The snow swirled around us. Tim tried to figure out how to dislodge the vehicle and get us back to the road. The only way we could distinguish the road was by the higher ridges of drifted snow on either side. One thing became clear to us—we were nowhere near the road and we couldn't drive the Renault back to it. It wouldn't be long before the swirling snow covered us so that if any cars came our way they wouldn't be able to see us.

We both stood outside the Renault, unable to figure out what to do.

Tim looked at me and took my hands. He began what would likely be our last prayer together. His last words were: "It's been a good life, Lord, and we don't have any regrets. If You're finished with us, it's okay. But if You can still use us, spare us now."

Just as Tim finished praying, he yelled, "I think I see something. Could it be. . . ?"

I saw it too. The best I could tell, a distant figure trudged our way, but as my vision cleared I saw that it wasn't one man, but three walking in single file. They were tall and muscular.

The men walked right up to the car. They didn't speak. One of them lightly nudged Tim aside and took his place at the rear. One man bent forward on the left side of the car and the other on the right. As if they had some silent signal among them, they picked up the Renault, carried it to the road, and set it down.

"Give them some money," I called out to Tim.

Before he could react, they were gone.

"But where did they go?" I asked. "We could see them coming. So why can't we see them leaving?"

"They weren't just men."

We completed our journey to Sofia, praising God throughout the final miles. Even though the storm didn't diminish, the car didn't slip or slide.

Why would we have any further problems? God sent three of His angels to deliver us. They had saved our lives, so their job was done.

CHAPTER TWELVE

Bicycle Angel

Delores E. Topliff

I'm sorry, Delores. There's no food in the house except for one can of corn and another of green beans." Mom took me aside before leaving for work that morning. As she had most days, she looked tired and defeated. "I can't buy anything until payday, and that's five days away. I don't know what you'll give the kids for dinner."

The strain of separation from Dad, financial problems, and the exhaustion of standing on her feet all day working in a potato-chip factory showed in her face. I hugged her. "Don't worry," I said, wanting to believe my own words. "Something will work out."

Mom smiled wanly and left for work.

At fifteen, I was the oldest girl, followed by my sister Nancy, almost nine, and our little brother Stu, nearly three. I couldn't discuss the problem with them, but I could talk to God about it. I had put my trust in Him three years earlier at summer camp, and my life was better after that. Although the rest of my family weren't Christians, I learned that Jesus cares for me and helps me even when things are hard. I also believed that asking God for food would be an opportunity to show my family that He answers prayers and would do something for us we couldn't do for ourselves.

"Jesus, please bring us food today because we don't have any. And do it so Mom will know that You're real." I was at peace, certain that God was going to provide food for us.

Nancy and I started Saturday housecleaning, but I kept peeping out our front window to see how and when our answer would come.

A little before noon, a man, who was probably in his sixties, rode a well-used blue Schwinn bicycle down our street. He turned into the driveway to our house. Neatly dressed, he wore blue work pants, a crisp white shirt open at the neck, and a faded dark derby hat. Although I hadn't seen him before, he looked sweet and cheerful, so I felt no hesitation in opening our door.

Smiling pleasantly, he pulled three white three-by-five cards from a pack of them in his shirt pocket. He greeted me and then asked, "Have you noticed the brand-new grocery store built on Mill Plain Boulevard about a mile from here?"

"I've seen it, but haven't been there yet."

"Today's their grand opening." He smiled and added, "They're celebrating by giving gift cards to a few customers that entitle them to groceries." He handed me the three white cards he held in his hand. "These are for you."

In the past, when new businesses opened in our neighborhood, it meant free balloons, coffee, or punch, and sometimes a cookie or two. One new business gave away gorgeous baby orchids with each gasoline fill-up.

I stared at the cards, amazed as I read what they offered. The first entitled us to a free gallon of milk; the second, to a jumbo loaf of bread; and the third to a half gallon of top-quality ice cream–any flavor.

I read the words out loud, and behind me Nancy and Stu began yelling and clapping.

"Thank you." I probably would have said more but my mind was on those three cards. And they were free.

The old man smiled again and his blue eyes twinkled. He waved good-bye and climbed back on his bicycle. He wobbled down our drive-way and rode up our street until he turned the corner and disappeared from sight. I watched but didn't see him stop at any other house.

Can this be true? I asked myself. Were these cards really good for groceries? I reminded myself that I had prayed for Jesus to bring us food. It seemed a little strange to come that way. I wanted to rush to the store immediately.

I had one problem. I couldn't leave the kids home alone, so I got my bike out of the garage, put my little brother in the wire basket on the front, and balanced my sister on the seat behind me. Her arms held tightly around my waist while I pedaled the mile to the grocery store.

Once there, it was safe to leave the bicycle in front, so I parked and took my sister and brother inside with me. The store was crowded with shoppers. I stood back. I was shy and hesitant to ask a clerk about our cards. When there was a break between customers, I walked over to a checkout clerk. "A man came to our house a while ago and gave us these cards." I held them up for her to see. "He said they're good for free groceries, no purchase necessary, since it's your grand opening. Is that right?"

Her answer seemed to take forever, but she soon nodded, smiled and said, "Yes, indeed. You're entitled to the groceries printed on the card. No cost. Go find what you want, and when you're through, come back to me."

My sister and brother and I walked around the store having fun as they helped me choose the items. We selected a gallon of whole milk in a plastic jug, a jumbo loaf of sliced white bread, and we agreed on a half-gallon of Cherry Garden Delight ice cream with walnuts.

When I brought them to the checkout, the nice clerk took our three gift cards, bagged our selections and smiled at us. We didn't see anyone else with white cards.

I wasn't sure I could pedal home with the extra load, but I was determined to try. I piled Stu in the bike's basket and carefully packed the groceries around him. Nancy climbed on behind me and held tight again as I pedaled home.

We were excited, and I felt as rich as a king.

Back at our house, I searched the kitchen cupboards again, and found a partial bag of macaroni crammed into a back corner and a can of stewed tomatoes on a bottom shelf.

By the time Mom came home from work, I had added those ingredients to the canned corn and green beans to make a huge bowl of steaming goulash for our table. Glasses of fresh milk stood alongside each plate, along with a saucer of sliced bread and a dessert bowl for ice cream.

"Where did all this food come from?" Mom's face lit up–the happiest I'd seen her in a long time. "You didn't have anything when I left."

I told her I prayed and afterward God sent a man on a bicycle with gift cards for free groceries from the new store. I told her I took the kids with me on my bike and the cards really were good for the things on our table and it didn't cost us any money.

Mom shook her head as we held hands before eating to pray, telling God, "Thank You." Mom saw that God had clearly answered my prayer and provided for us abundantly.

I'll never forget that meal and the atmosphere of well-being we felt around our table that night eating food provided by heaven. Our little family sat warmed by God's love, and I believe Mom worried less after that.

Monday morning at our school bus stop, I questioned the other kids waiting at the corner. "Did a man on a bicycle come to your house Saturday with gift cards from the new grocery store? Did you see someone ride down the street and come to our house? Did you see anyone on a bicycle?"

No matter who I asked, all of them said no. That surprised me, because most of the kids on our street seemed to see everything that went on. None of them had seen an old man on a bicycle.

Was he really just a sweet old man, wearing tidy work clothes and a faded hat, who rode a bicycle and personally answered prayers? Or was he an angel–a heavenly messenger–sent to answer my prayers?

I don't know. And it doesn't make any difference. We were a family in need, I prayed for food, and God answered. Human or divine being–it was truly a messenger from God who provided food for us until Mom had money once again.

CHAPTER THIRTEEN

Breathe

Heather Marsten

After we got home from juvenile court, the reality of what happened sunk in. I was placed in the custody of my sister Diane and her husband Bobby. My father couldn't abuse me anymore. I was fifteen years old.

I'm safe, I told myself several times.

Diane cleared out two dresser drawers and half the closet in the room I would share with their daughter Connie. I started unpacking and grabbed a hanger for my blue plaid skirt. *I really don't have to go back there.*

While I put my socks in the drawer, I thought about the notebooks my mom kept of my father's sexually abusing me–notebooks the courts used for evidence. For a long time she was afraid to do anything, but she wrote down everything I told her. *Did Mommy get beaten for writing them?*

After I finished unpacking, I sat on my side of the bed in Connie's room. *I prayed that someone would rescue me, and it's happened.* I put my head in my hands. *I should be grateful and glad, but I'm still scared.*

Before getting ready for bed I went to the family room and asked my sister, "Should I take a bath or a shower?" I'd never had to make that kind of decision before. Dad always told me when I needed to do anything.

"Come on, Heather. A grown kid like you can't decide? Even Connie at age eight can figure that one out for herself. You'd better start growing up."

The next day I registered at my new school and began to make friends. For once, I felt as if I was normal and living in a normal environment. I relaxed and took interest in school life.

Two months later Diane called me into her room. "We have to talk."

My stomach seemed to jump to my throat. *What did I do wrong?* She shut the door, and we sat on her bed.

"Because Bobby and I work, you're going to have to help out around here. I've made a chart of daily chores for you. I've made one for Connie too."

"Okay." I read the list. It wasn't too bad, just a job a day like cleaning the bathroom, laundry, vacuuming, and dishes. "It seems fair."

Then she shocked me by saying, "I don't know what's wrong with you. You have to start acting normal. You walk around looking like a whipped dog all the time."

It's only been two months since I got out of that house. What do you expect? "I'll try–"

"Tell me what Daddy really did to you."

Perhaps because of my father and the past abuse, I felt I needed to be careful, so I told her what Mommy wrote in the notebooks. There were other things–worse things–but I didn't feel safe in telling her.

Diane didn't say anything until I finished. Then she stared at me and said, "You must have done something to encourage him if he went that far with you."

What? Don't you remember that none of us ever said no to Daddy? "I didn't encourage him," I said and could feel my words choking me. "He told me he'd kill me if I didn't do what he wanted."

"He's a dirty, no-good jerk." She may have said more but that's all I remember. She got up, took off her watch and started to remove her jewelry. She acted as if we had had only a normal sister-to-sister conversation. "I have to take a shower. Why don't you go set the table?"

How could she change that much? I thought that she, of all people, should understand.

At dinner Connie dropped her fork and spilled food on the floor. Diane slapped her, and Connie started to cry.

"Shut up," Diane yelled and wiped the spot on the floor. She practically threw a clean fork at her daughter. "If you don't quit crying, you'll get it harder next time."

I stared at my plate and ate my meatballs. *It's beginning to look a lot like home here.*

I wanted Diane to like me. I tried my hardest to please her, but I realized then—as I probably should have noticed from the first days in her house—she got angry at the least little thing.

If Diane is so much like Daddy, there is no escape for me. I don't want to grow up to be like him. After dinner, I put away the dishes. That's when I spotted Diane's pain medicine on the top shelf. I counted fifteen out-of-date prescription bottles. I decided to take some. I stole eight pills, the most I felt I could unobtrusively take.

"I might as well swallow the pills and die," I whispered to myself.

After everyone was asleep, I sneaked into the kitchen for a glass of water. I stared at the pills in my palm. I hesitated for several seconds. *Do I really want to do this? Why not? Death is better than what I'm dealing with now.*

I took the pills along with twenty aspirin for good measure. My only regret was that Connie would probably be the first one to find me dead in the morning. But I hurt so much I couldn't take any more of Diane's yelling at me.

I lay on my bed and waited for the pills to take effect and kill me. The room spun, and my stomach churned. I felt nausea and fought it, determined not to throw up the pills. I finally chewed a stick of gum to stop myself from gagging.

Before long, I gasped for breath and told myself, "Breathe." But at the same time I wondered, *Why am I fighting for life? I want to die.*

The floor seemed to heave like the deck of a ship during a storm. I grabbed the side of my bed, trying to still the waves of nausea and pain that engulfed me.

My throat locked up, and I couldn't call for help. "God, if You are there, if You care about me, help. I don't want to die. I thought I did, but I don't."

I gasped for breath. *It would be so easy not to struggle*, I thought. So easy not to breathe, just sink into the void.

Someone sat next to me on my bed. I was so nauseated, I couldn't open my eyes. I stopped breathing. If this is what death is, it's not so bad.

A man's voice said, "Breathe in, breathe out. Breathe in, breathe out."

I didn't stop to think about who was talking to me. Obediently, I took a deep breath and let it out. Each time the voice said, "Breathe in," I did.

I don't know how long that lasted. It seemed like hours. The soothing voice repeated, "Breathe in, breathe out."

When morning came, the room finally stopped spinning and I was able to breathe naturally.

I opened my eyes, but the man was gone.

I have no doubts that God sent an angel to keep me alive. That happened a long time ago. I lived and stayed with my sister until I was able to get out on my own.

Today, I've been married for twenty-five years and have three grown children. Without that angelic visit, I would never have known the happiness I have now.

In my dark moments, I can go back to that night. I can still hear that deep voice telling me to breathe, hour after hour. It amazes me that God would go to such extraordinary lengths to keep me alive.

CHAPTER FOURTEEN

Careful–An Angel Is Watching

Shirley A. Reynolds

It was my first night doing evangelistic outreach. I walked with my staff leader to an area called Market Plaza. From 9:00 AM until 5:00 PM, the plaza was a bustling stream of activity for working people. After 9:00 PM street youth filled the area.

As we walked together, four obvious gang members, dressed in red gang colors, approached us.

"Stay close and listen to what I say," my leader whispered.

"No problem," I said, even though I was already frightened.

What am I doing here? I pictured myself as Ms. Susie Suburbia, dressed in clean clothes and every hair in place. I am so out of my comfort zone. But I reminded myself, this is what I'd wanted to do.

My leader stopped and talked to the group of four. Everyone seemed to ignore me. Just then, someone touched my arm. I turned and stared at a medium-built man, who was dressed in a suit, white shirt, and tie, and had an infectious smile. He held a cane in one hand. With his other hand, he held a rose and handed me the flower.

"Hello," he said. "My name is Charlie, and I'm here to tell you that you'll do well here. You have the love of Jesus in your heart. And never forget: God takes away all fears, even your fear of the street youth. He called you and is with you."

"How do you know those things?" I asked.

"I know, because God is with you."

"But your clothes. Your smile. You don't fit in this place."

The staff leader said good-bye to the gang members, and we walked down the dark street. I turned to him, "Did you see that man?" I asked, "Do you know who he is?"

"What man are you talking about?" I tried to explain, but he said, "No one talked to you. I was right here and I'd have known."

"But he was right beside me," I said and held up the rose. "He gave this to me."

"There was no man standing here."

I insisted there was, so he smiled and said, "All right, let's find your person. Who knows? Maybe he was your guardian angel."

Clutching the rose in my hand, I followed. We looked in the entryways of several abandoned buildings and searched the street. We never found Charlie.

I kept silent about Charlie and the rose. But I was different. Charlie had told me that God takes away all fears. I realized I was no longer afraid. After that, I thought of Charlie as my guardian angel.

A few weeks later, while eating a cinnamon roll inside a corner bakery called the Muffin Man, I spotted a homeless lady in the opening of a building across the street. It was a damp morning, and I wondered if she would enjoy breakfast.

After purchasing an extra roll and a hot chocolate, I hurried across the street. Kneeling down on the concrete in front of her, I said, "Would you like some breakfast? I saw you from the window. This is the first time I've seen you here, but I'll come back every morning if you are here. How does that sound?"

Without a word, she grabbed the bag and began to pull off bites of the roll. I set the hot chocolate close to her, and with one bony hand she lifted it up to drink.

She didn't speak, and I wondered if she was the bag lady my staff called "Muted Annie." I had to leave for work, but before I left I said, "I need to go now. I'd like to tell you that Jesus loves you. I *will* be back tomorrow."

I kept my word. I met with her every morning for several weeks. She was Annie and finally spoke. We talked about street life. One day she invited me to sit on her sleeping bag. In the middle of broken wine bottles and the smell of urine, we shared our lives.

One morning, I asked her if I could pray for her, and she said I could. I showed her a large-print Bible, a glow-in-the-dark cross, and a flashlight for her dark nights.

"These are yours," I said.

She took them and bowed her head for the prayer. Long wisps of gray hair fell from under her hood. I noticed her broken teeth, but her words were beautiful. "God, if You are there," she began, "come in this haggled old woman's heart. I've got a lot of bad things in my heart. Just let me know that You love me."

I grabbed her thin hands and began to pray. "Lord, You know how long Annie has struggled. Please let her know that You love her, and You forgive every sin she's ever committed."

We both cried.

She smiled, and as I stood to leave, I turned and said, "See you tomorrow."

Smiling, she whispered, "Maybe it'll be tonight God comes for me. What do you think?"

"Who knows but God?" I said, and trudged up the hill.

The next day, I followed the same routine. Rain poured as I ran across the street with the tasty food. Without looking, I ran into Annie's hovel and stopped. Her sleeping bag was torn into shreds. Her garbage bag of tin cans was ripped open and every can was smashed. Her umbrella was broken in pieces, and her Bible, cross, and flashlight were gone. Tears filled my eyes.

"Hey, what are you doing?" a man called. "Are you that outreach worker that met Annie every morning?"

I turned around. A homeless man sat on a park bench. He was dressed in overalls, a thin T-shirt, and sandals. He shivered as he spoke. "Annie was beat up and killed last night. I saw it all. I was hiding behind that dumpster." He pointed to it. "But I heard her mumble something. Sounded like, 'I see him. I see him. He's coming down Main Street.' Does that mean anything to you?"

Wiping the tears from my eyes, I said, "Oh yes. It means something to me."

The man handed me Annie's Bible and the cross.

"Mind if I keep the flashlight?" he asked.

"No, of course not," I whispered, as I looked at her Bible and cross. "Here, why don't you keep Annie's Bible? Do you know that Jesus loved Annie, and He loves you too?"

"Who me? A dirty, old alcoholic?"

"God can work miracles on dirty, old alcoholics," I said, and handed him the bag of cinnamon rolls and the hot chocolate.

"I'll be here every morning, if you are. And I'll bring you breakfast."

"I'll be here," he said.

As I turned to go, I said, "One day you're going to look up Main Street, and Jesus will be coming for you."

"Yeah, yeah," he said.

I crossed the street and leaned against the wall of an abandoned building. I opened my hand to look at the glow-in-the-dark cross.

"Oh, God, take care of Annie. I'll miss her."

Before I hurried up the hill to the drop-in center, I stole another look at the corner where Annie had lived. My heart seemed to stop beating as I stared. I rubbed my eyes, but the person was still standing in her corner. In the midst of the rubble, there stood Charlie, all dressed up. He was smiling, and I smiled back.

When I blinked, the image was gone.

I don't know how to explain all of this and I'm not a person who sees visions or imagines people. But I know Charlie was real. I could never have stayed out on the streets reaching out to the homeless if he hadn't taken away my fears.

But as I think of Annie and my new friend Tom, I remember Charlie's promise that I would do good things on the street.

Thank you, Charlie. Maybe you were an angel. Maybe you were a real person. It no longer matters. You came to me when I needed you. And I'm sure you came to Annie too.

CHAPTER FIFTEEN

Do Angels Carry Cash?

Kathleen Kohler

H ello, Violet," I said when one of our customers entered
the Christian gift and bookstore where I worked.

A regular shopper at the store, Violet wore her usual powder-blue sweater, lace-trimmed blouse, and gray slacks. Her black hand-bag hung over her left forearm, her white hair combed to its natural wave. The only thing missing was her bright smile.

"You remember my husband passed away two months ago?"
she asked. "Our grandson feels lost without him."

Violet told me her husband had prayed daily for their sixteen-year-old grandson, and that they had shared a close relationship.
With a catch in her throat she said, "Joshua wonders who will pray

for him now." His grief brought Violet into the store. "I'm hunting for something to cheer him up."

Together we searched the store shelves for just the right gift to help ease his pain. "What about this?" After several minutes I pointed to a framed painting of a boy carrying a backpack through a darkened forest. Light shone through the trees and radiated from an angel who watched over the young boy's path. Violet and I stood side by side and stared up at the eighteen-by-twenty-inch picture, titled "Never Alone."

"That would be perfect," Violet said. "If only I had that much money."

I hesitated. Though we had no coupons advertised, I said, "For you, Violet, I believe there's a special twenty percent discount today."

"That's nice of you, but it's still more than I can afford." With her head down, she confided, "I only have twenty dollars to spend. Thirty, if I dip into my household money."

On several occasions during my nearly eight years of managing the store I'd made up the difference when a customer fell short and had a real need. But this time I had no money to spare.

Just then, a chilled November wind swept through the front door and rattled the stained glass suncatcher display as a thirty-something man and a girl about eight years old entered the store. I greeted them with a smile and said, "I'll be right with you."

"No hurry," the man said. He was dressed in a long tan trench coat. He stepped over and stood behind us while the girl waited at the counter. "Nice picture," he said to Violet. "Are you going to buy that?"

"Well," she paused, and then went on to tell him her dilemma.

He nodded as he listened with a look of genuine compassion on his face. When she finished her story, he said, "I'll pay the balance."

Violet raised a gentle protest. "I couldn't let you do that," she said. "I don't even know who you are. And I certainly shouldn't have shared my troubles."

Pointing to the young girl, who I assumed was his daughter, he said, "We simply enjoy helping people. She's always giving food to someone. Besides, you said this picture is perfect for your grandson."

"Yes, I think it is. I believe that every time Joshua sees the angel it will remind him that even though Grandpa is gone, he's not alone."

"That settles it then," the man said. He took the picture from the wall, handed it to me, and said, "Wrap it up, please."

He and the girl oversaw the whole operation while I retrieved a box from the back room and removed the price tag. Violet stood in front of the counter next to the pair, her hands clutched together, tears glistening in her eyes. "This is so good of you," she said to the stranger several times.

I rang the price into the register and subtracted the promised twenty-percent off special. Violet set her twenty-dollar bill on the counter. "That leaves seventy-nine dollars," I said as I looked up at the man, who paid in cash.

I handed the box to Violet, and the man said, "I'll carry that. Is that your blue car out front?"

"Yes it is." He told the girl to wait inside for him and went outside with Violet.

When he returned, I asked if I could help him with a purchase. He thought for a moment. He appeared to have no clear reason for his visit to the store. In what seemed more like an afterthought, he decided to purchase a card. He snatched one up from the card rack, barely giving it a glance. The girl took a small forty-nine-cent metal cross from a basket by the register.

"We'll take these," he said and pushed them across the counter. With a big smile, the brown-haired girl told me how they were always on the lookout for people who needed help.

I thanked him for helping Violet. He paid for their items and they left the store. I glanced away for only a moment and when I looked up I expected to see them on the store's walkway. Then I realized Violet's had been the only car parked by the curb. With no sign of the man and the girl, I rushed to the huge windows that fronted the entire store. Puzzled when I still didn't see them, I ran out to the curb and looked up and down the sidewalk. They had simply vanished.

I knew most of my customers at the bookstore by name, or at least I recognized their faces. But not that curious pair–I had never seen them before. Apparently their only purpose for visiting the store that day was to help an older woman encourage her grandson. Whether they were Good Samaritans or angels, I never saw them again.

I've often thought that their coming at exactly the right time to help Violet in her need was an example of God's perfect timing. Were they just two strangers who liked to help others? Or were they more than that?

CHAPTER SIXTEEN

Heavenly Company

Virginia Garberding

Over the last years I had prayed many times after visiting my folks, "Dear Lord, I don't know how this can end well. Mom is in the nursing home and Dad, who has always been there for her, is now failing fast. His memory problems are becoming so much more apparent. You know how fearful Dad is of Alzheimer's disease. He's always been a bad patient and now he dreads the possibility of having to be dressed, fed, bathed, and becoming dependent. I've seen this many times before with others, I don't see how this can end well. Help us, Lord."

In the weeks after Dad had the stroke, he remained in a coma. My brother Marty and his wife, Mary, agreed to share the vigil. I took the day shift and they took the nights. The time seemed to fly, with pastors, church members, and people from the nursing home coming daily. I passed the days reading to Dad from the Bible and singing. I especially liked singing his favorites, "How Great Thou Art" and "Heaven Is My Home."

At night, when my brother came in for the switch of shifts, Mary said. "I'm so glad to be here for Dad. I never was able to do this for my folks."

After a week, the hospital sent a nurse from hospice to talk to me and give me papers to fill out before the transfer to a hospice unit the next morning.

Standing there with the doctor who had come from intensive care because he had heard that Dad was "someone important," I said, "Yes, he was a pastor."

I asked the doctor, "How long can a person last like this without food or water?"

The doctor took a long look at Dad, the still clear urine in his drainage bag and lack of respiratory distress and said, "It's going to be a few days yet."

After the doctor left, I was determined to get down to that paperwork, because we needed it the next morning. But realizing that it was now after 6:00 PM. I decided to call my sister, knowing she would be home from work and waiting for the day's update.

I went over to the large window ledge and leaned toward the window, where I knew I would have the best reception with my cell phone. As I was telling her what the doctor said, I sensed a movement behind me. I turned around, knowing Dad had stopped moving several days before.

The door was closed, no one had peeked inside to see if I wanted anything, and Dad was lying there just as still as before. I turned back to stare into the night sky and that's when I saw a reflection in the window of something behind me.

I wanted to see if there was an obvious or natural explanation for the heavenly phenomena I witnessed in that hospital room. I quickly looked down the five floors to see if there was any way something was shining up to that room. Below I saw only the typical street traffic coming and going to the hospital. Nothing unusual there.

As I turned and looked behind me, my first thought was, *Oh, it's you.*

The memory came flashing back. In October 1987, I was the night nurse on a Medicare floor, sitting there at four in the morning charting. I looked up at various times to watch the three nursing assistants walk back and forth across the dimly lit hall in front of me as they went to change linen and turn debilitated patients.

The next sight was strange. I watched the three come out of one room, cross the hall in single file and go into the next room. They did this several times, but I looked up and there were *four* of them.

The fourth figure was much taller than the other three and towered above them. He was a man, but he didn't so much walk as glide across the hall. I can't describe him, but he was extremely tall and slow moving.

As I sat there, I thought, *They walk with angels and don't know it.* Should I tell them?

I didn't say anything that night. But over the years that sight never diminished from my memory. Whenever I had a chance to do so, I would tell caregivers, "You know you walk with angels." They may not have grasped what I meant, but I knew.

In the back of my mind I often wondered why God had allowed me to see the angel that night, but as I sat beside my father, I suddenly understood. It was so I wouldn't be afraid and I'd be clear about what I was seeing.

As I watched, that tall man from years earlier was there. I knew it was an angel; and as he passed directly over Dad, I was once again caught up in his large size and the slow graceful movements.

I now knew why I saw what I had seen in 1987, and why I saw it now. It was for my comfort. I felt a great sense of peace. As the angel appeared to pass right through the wall, I knew I wouldn't be able to see it again.

I turned back to the window. I didn't tell my sister what I had just seen but said simply, "Dad will be gone tonight." She never questioned how I knew.

When Marty and Mary came for their nightly vigil, I also told them, "Dad will be gone tonight." I knew that God had not only spared Dad from the life he had been so much dreading, but He had given me what I didn't know I needed–comfort and deep-settled peace.

I left those hospice papers untouched on the night stand. I took a last long gaze around the room so I would always remember the look and feel of that night.

Marty sat in his usual place next to the bed. Dad was peaceful and still, his breathing regular as though he were sleeping. Mary leaned over him, whispering, "Take Jesus' hand, Dad. Take Jesus' hand."

I said "Good-bye, Dad," for the last time and left. He died shortly after I left the hospital.

The ninety-minute ride home that night was different from the previous seven. The feeling of comfort, peace, and knowledge of how senseless worry is has stayed with me every day for the past six years since Dad died. When trouble comes, in whatever form—standing next to my car with a flat tire, hearing of a loved one diagnosed with cancer, or family conflicts—I take it to the Lord and leave it there because I know He can and will handle it.

After Dad died, I didn't tell everyone I had seen an angel. Just like many years earlier, I would mention it whenever someone seemed to need to know. As time passed, I read Bible passages referencing angels and read a few books about people seeing angels. But I consciously didn't want to be caught up in the pursuit of angels. However, I have taken much pleasure in the thought that nurses are referred to as "angels of mercy."

CHAPTER SEVENTEEN

The Night Visitor

Grace G. Booth

My parents, my sister Nelly, and I all returned to the States after our missionary trip in Haiti. We settled in Des Allemands, Louisiana, a bayou village about ninety miles west of New Orleans. Dad said he saw a need and felt that God led us to move there.

Because they were French-speaking, my parents assumed ministering to the Cajun people would be a natural fit. They were mistaken; the Cajun culture looked suspiciously at outsiders.

Although the majority of the residents spoke French, their Cajun didn't connect with the French Dad had learned in his home in New York City. Mom, a French national, spoke "funny French" to our Cajun neighbors.

My parents refused to be discouraged. Several times Dad said, "This is where God wants us to be." Unable to find a staff position in a local church, however, Dad searched for work. For a long time, he found nothing permanent.

Nelly and I attended the local elementary school. In time, of course, classmates accepted us. Our family slowly integrated into Louisiana life, and Dad found a permanent position.

We were just beginning to feel we belonged there, when Mom got sick. Her face began to swell. Each day the swelling increased.

A neighbor gasped when she saw Mom. "You've got to go to the hospital right away!"

We had no money for hospitals or doctor visits, but Dad knew how to pray. "God will take care of us," he told Nelly and me so we wouldn't worry. "I intend to pray all night for your mother's healing."

That night, while Dad prayed, Nelly and I went to sleep in the small pass-through bedroom at the center of the house.

I was startled awake with the sense of someone else being in the room with Nelly and me. Through the faint light, I could barely discern a figure–head and shoulders and the rest of the body draped in a translucent robe.

Fearfully, I hid my face under the sheet and waited for a long time before peeking out. The figure followed my father as he walked through the room praying silently. Dad flipped on the light in the kitchen and the strange creature disappeared.

Although I wondered what it was, I was no longer afraid. I went back to sleep.

The next morning at the breakfast table, Nelly asked Dad, "Did you see the angel last night?"

"No, but I felt its presence," he said and smiled at her.

As they talked, I realized that our visitor was an angel.

Nelly said the figure spread his arms over our bed before following Dad as he paced.

The swelling on Mom's face disappeared. The night visitor not only brought healing to our mom, but a deep peace to all of us.

Nearly sixty years have passed since that night visitor came to us. In those moments when doubts come or I face intense problems, I remind myself of that angelic presence. Then I smile to myself. God *is* with me.

CHAPTER EIGHTEEN

An Angel in Scrubs

Andrea Arthur Owan

O*h, God, why must I continue to suffer in this dark valley? Why couldn't this birth be easy?*

For the second time in my pregnancy, I battled premature labor. After twenty-two weeks, I endured surgery to close my cervix. Then I was confined to bed for three months. Spiritual battles intensified as the months progressed. My body was being pumped full of ineffective sedatives and contraction-ending drugs. My unborn baby was unresponsive, and my mental stamina eroded along with my physical state.

Now, in my seventh month, I was alone in a dark hospital room. And terrified of the outcome.

Almost two years earlier, our precious daughter Victoria died during a delivery that almost ended my life as well. My husband Chris and I had grieved deeply and struggled to recover. We had prayed earnestly until we were certain God was with us and we should try again.

I closed my eyes and returned to a favorite prayer by James Dillet Freeman that I had learned:

The light of God surrounds me;

The love of God enfolds me;

The power of God protects me;

The presence of God watches over me.

Wherever I am, God is.

Over and over I repeated it, with additional fervor during the worst waves of breath-stopping contractions. It helped me to focus on the loving presence of Jesus.

My doctor, who monitored my condition and gave directions from his home, seemed unresponsive to my distress. Medication levels elevated repeatedly as my contractions worsened.

Already fearful, I grew even more concerned for the effect of the drugs on my unborn baby.

At six the next morning, contractions still crushed against my pelvis. I gripped my pillow and repeated my prayer more intensely.

My nurse evaluated the monitor yet another time. She said nothing, but she seemed nervous and left abruptly.

Only minutes later, my doctor called on my bedside phone. "I think it's time to hang this one up. I'm going to stop the medication," he said. "When I get there, I'll cut the stitches and let whatever happens, happen. I think we'll be having a baby here within the next several hours."

Excitedly I called Chris. "Hurry to the hospital," I said and repeated what the doctor had told me. One of the nurses notified the Neonatal Intensive Care Unit that a six-and-a-half-month preemie would likely be delivered in a few hours. The nurses seemed extremely excited.

The contractions came and each one seemed harder. But by six-thirty the pain bordered on unbearable. "Oh, dear Jesus," I choked, "please help me bear my burden. You took me through this once before, so please help me again. Please."

Suddenly an unrelenting contraction slammed my body. Terror pierced me. The next contraction escalated ferociously, and the sutures ruptured.

My baby was arriving in a dark, lonesome hospital room.

Hysterical, I screamed for someone to help me. As my nurse hurried into the room, I wailed, "It's here. My baby's here."

"Stop pushing!" She placed one hand on my unborn baby's head. She called for help through the wall intercom. Within seconds a barrage of nurses swarmed in, and a call went to the NICU.

My doctor hadn't arrived, so someone on staff called an emergency room doctor. We waited, and I prayed in hyperventilating jerks. For ten minutes, a nurse kept my baby from complete delivery before the doctor suddenly appeared and stared aghast at the chaotic scene.

"Is there a heartbeat?" I asked several times.

No one answered. The monitor had slipped, and everyone had forgotten about checking the baby's condition. Quickly and calmly my doctor instructed me to push gently. Three times I obediently followed his order.

Finally, my baby was born.

"It's a boy," a nurse squealed.

Before long, I was able to sit up and take in the beautiful vision of my newborn baby. He lay absolutely still and lifeless on the bed; his little form in a dreadful hue of blue.

Collapsing on the pillow, I dragged a wet washcloth over my face and mumbled into the damp cotton, "Oh, God, I can't lose another one. I just can't lose another baby. Please don't make me go through this again. I thought I could, but I can't."

Just then, a nurse I didn't recognize grabbed my right hand and arm, leaned over me, and began praying magnificent words of power and conviction. Her voice was soothing, and I felt instant gratefulness for her presence.

"Are you a Christian?" she asked matter-of-factly.

"I certainly am." I stared at the young woman who had appeared so suddenly. She continued to pray while puffing up my pillows and cleaned the area around my head and arms. I couldn't seem to take my gaze off her. Each gesture felt like a silent signal for more inner peace.

I wasn't the only one staring at her. Other nurses observed her somewhat questioningly, as if they didn't recognize her or understand why she was there. She ignored them and continued to smile and talk softly to me.

"Is he breathing?" I asked.

"They're working on him," came the reserved and succinct reply from a voice near my bed. Everyone seemed busy while anxiously waiting for some noise to escape from the baby warmer in the corner where a team of NICU nurses blocked my view.

A hush, stretching like eternity, filled the room.

"Is he breathing yet?" Feeling as if I would crack from the choking volume of silence, I asked again.

"They're still working on him," another nurse said without meeting my eyes.

I was ready to ask yet again when a beautiful, tiny cry emitted from the table over which the group huddled. A cheer erupted from the staff as the team whisked my son to the NICU. In that instant, the terror, the bottled-up emotions, doubts, and anguish dissolved. My baby had arrived. He was real; he was breathing. I knew he would be fine.

My gaze scrutinized the room, seeking the face of my praying nurse. She was gone. She hadn't said anything—not a single parting word before she left.

Vera, a nurse who had cared for me during the first bout of premature labor three months earlier, stayed to change my pillows, remove my IV, and return the room to some semblance of order.

When the two of us were alone together, I asked, "Who was that nurse? The one who prayed?"

"I don't know. I've never seen her before." She stopped and stared at me. "I've worked here a long time. Maybe she came from the emergency room. Would you like me to find out?"

"Yes, please. I'd like to thank her."

"I'll order breakfast for you, get some clean towels for your shower, and ask around."

"Thank you."

Within half an hour she returned. "I asked the nurses in the emergency department, and they'd never seen her before. They thought it was strange too. No one I talked to has ever seen her before."

"You're saying that she just came, prayed for me, and then disappeared?"

"Kind of strange, isn't it?"

I nodded. Nothing more needed to be said.

Vera left, and I lay in bed, once again staring at the ceiling. *Could it be, God? Could You have sent an angel just for me? An angel in nurse's scrubs? Or a dedicated nurse moved to deliver comfort to a weak, terrified mother?*

God had walked me through a blackened valley and onto a mountaintop. If the birth had been easy, would I have missed His miraculous love, provision, and power? Thankfulness and awe of my loving God engulfed me. I closed my eyes and wept.

Now years later, whenever I remember that day, I wonder anew. And I'm humbled. Regardless of whether it was a human being or an angel (which is what I believe), I know that God sent that messenger—that ministering spirit—to meet my need.

CHAPTER NINETEEN

Ice Water in the Desert

Helen L. Hoover

O h no. What do we do?" Steam rolled out from under the hood of our car. As quickly as possible, my husband Larry pulled to the side of the road. We were on Interstate 15 in an isolated area midway between Barstow, California, and Las Vegas.

Heat rose in waves from the hot concrete to assault us when we stepped outside the car. Barren desert surrounded us. Larry raised the hood and said, "The radiator hose burst."

"What do we do?" I asked again.

"We passed a sign that said there's a service station ahead. I'll go and see if they have radiator hoses and be back in a little bit."

Our two sons and I watched Larry walking toward the station until he was out of sight on that unbearably hot Sunday afternoon.

"Do you suppose they'll have a hose to fit our car?" fifteen-year-old Grant asked.

"What will we do if they don't?" eight-year-old Gary asked.

Their questions went unanswered. I said little but prayed for Larry to find exactly what we needed.

About an hour after he left, Larry returned with the rubber hose. "It was expensive, but who are we to argue about price at this point?"

He easily replaced the burst hose. "Grant, get the gallon of water out of the trailer. That should last until we get to the station where we can fill the radiator."

Larry drove slowly to the service station. It had several coin-operated water pumps for their customers' use. Larry drove to one of the water pumps, got out, and raised the hood. The gallon of water in the radiator had heated to boiling and was under tremendous pressure. Without thinking, Larry unscrewed the radiator cap.

Boiling water erupted. Larry jumped back and turned his head, but not quick enough. In a split second, the water scalded the right side of his face.

Before I could get out to help, another car sped up to Larry's side. The driver rolled down his window and held out a pitcher filled with water and crushed ice. "Here, you need this," he said.

A tormented Larry grabbed the pitcher and poured the water on the burnt side of his face. The icy water gave momentary relief. He handed the empty pitcher back to the man, who took it. Without another word the car drove off.

I rushed to Larry. "How badly are you hurt?"

"Help me to the car."

Distraught, confused, and perplexed, we discussed our options. The closest medical help was seventy-five miles away. We didn't have anything suitable to put on his face. It was still fourteen hundred miles to our home.

After waiting for the radiator to cool down and filling it with water, I drove us to Las Vegas. Larry turned the air-conditioner vent to blow the cold air directly on his face and held a wet wash cloth on the burned side. He was in agony, and I couldn't do anything to help him.

As the shock of the event dissipated, we talked about the unusual incident of the man with the water container. The pitcher was clear glass, fish-bowl shaped, without a lid, like the ones used in restaurants. The water had crushed ice in it.

"You know, there wasn't a restaurant at the service station," Larry said.

"Not only that," I said, "but the man arrived before any of us could move or even yell for help."

"He didn't stay around, like people usually do," Grant said.

"How did he do that?" Gary asked. I wasn't sure what he meant so he said, "How did he carry a pitcher of ice water inside the car without spilling it?"

"You're right," I said. "No human would carry a full, open pitcher of ice water while driving a car and not spill any."

"Do you think he was an angel?" Grant asked.

"I didn't know angels drove cars," our other son said.

Later, Larry told me about the thoughts that went through his mind. "Even with my face screaming in pain," he said, "I knew I had put you in a precarious position. I wondered if I needed to go to a hospital and alter our vacation plans. All because I had made a stupid decision in unscrewing the radiator cap so quickly. I knew better." He didn't have to mention that for years he had often worked on cars.

By the time we arrived at Las Vegas, Larry's face wasn't hurting very much, so he didn't think we needed to find a hospital emergency room. Instead, we located a drug store and bought burn ointment. We traveled on to Zion National Park in Utah to camp for the night. With everyone helping, we set up the trailer. Larry immediately lay down for the night. From his face, I could tell that that he was exhausted.

Surprisingly, the next morning Larry's face didn't hurt.

"Are you sure you feel like driving?" I asked when he said we would continue our vacation plans and he would drive.

On the third day, the skin on the burnt side of Larry's face looked like the bottom of a dry, cracked pond.

The next day, Larry's face had the appearance of someone in a horror movie. One side had normal skin and the other side was haphazardly flaking off in dry pieces that lifted off like pie crust. Over the next two days, the burned skin continued to flake. By the time we arrived home in Missouri on Saturday evening, his face showed no signs of having been severely burned only six days earlier.

Twenty-eight years later, we continue to tell others of the unusual help God provided. We are awed at His provision.

Who was the man with the ice water? Where did he come from? How did he know about Larry's burn? It's a mystery to us, because we don't know the answer. That's all right because I'm convinced it was an angel–a ministering spirit–sent to us by God in a moment of need.

Since then, Hebrews 1:14 has become one of my favorite verses: "Angels are only servants–spirits sent to care for people who will inherit salvation."

CHAPTER TWENTY

The Voice to the Fisherman

Jeffrey Leach with Delilah Moore Leach

I was happy to have graduated from high school. I would work long hours during the summer to earn money for college in the fall. But today was mine, and I was going to go trout fishing, my favorite leisure-time activity.

I lived only seven miles from the Santiam River in western Oregon. The river, which fed two dams, provided excellent fishing opportunities, especially in the steep gorge between the two dams. This area wasn't readily accessible, so large rainbow trout lurked in its deep pools of crystal clear water.

As I followed the narrow, winding, five-mile stretch of road that had only one or two spots for cars to pull off, I looked for a place to park so I could make my way down to the river.

After I found a parking spot for my car, I grabbed my pole in one hand and my tackle box in the other and started down the steep embankment. I carefully edged my way down the slope until I reached a ledge. The water was low because the first dam had let out so much water that it exposed the rocky bank. I stood on the ledge staring at the large river rocks about thirty or forty feet below, trying to find a way to get down to the water.

The mossy rock on which I stood sloped toward the ledge and was surrounded by small brush and bushes. I surveyed the obstacle and saw what might be a faint trail leading down toward the river below. I needed only to get around the bushes in front of me. Carefully I sat down, still holding my pole and tackle box, and started to scoot around the bush.

Just then, the moss underneath me gave way, and I slid off the rock, over the ledge, and into the air for a free fall of at least thirty feet to the rocks below.

A voice called out, "Stand straight. Hands at your sides."

I didn't have time to think about who called to me, but instinctively I did just that and fell straight down. As I fell, I wondered what it was going to be like when I hit the ground.

I landed on my feet on the river rocks. The reality was worse than I could imagine. I still had my pole in my left hand and my tackle box in my right, but I dropped them right away as debilitating, knifelike pain shot through my ankles and up my legs. I screamed and cried as I slumped to the ground and lay there in agony.

Time passed while I lay there screaming. Eventually, however, the sharp agony subsided enough so I could focus my thoughts. I began to contemplate my predicament and wondered how I would get out of there. I looked up at the cliff from which I had fallen. How had I survived? I remembered reading in the paper two weeks earlier about a fisherman who had fallen off a cliff and died. It happened in this same area.

Although I had survived, I had hurt myself badly, and I was at the bottom of a cliff. The accident happened in 1972, and there were no cell phones then.

I had to get out of there by myself.

Using my fishing pole to help me, I crawled on my hands and knees to the left, over the sharp, gravel-like rocks and larger rounded rocks until I reached a less steep part of the hill. From there I crawled about five hundred yards and discovered an old road. After resting a few minutes, I tried to walk on the graveled, overgrown road but I couldn't. I screamed because sharp pain gripped me with each step. It was going to be an ordeal to reach my car.

As I struggled to keep going, two men appeared on the road ahead of me. Both were about my size.

"What happened?" one man asked.

"Can we help you?" the other said.

I told them my story and asked if they could help me to my car parked on the road above. One on either side, with my arms resting on their shoulders, they carried me to my car.

They offered more help, but I told them I could drive using my toes if they could get me inside the car. As I scooted into the car, I looked down at my feet and saw that my ankles were twice their normal size.

Finally I got up the courage to put enough pressure on my feet to drive. As I drove to town, I looked for the men's car but didn't see it. When I reached town and pulled up in front of the family business, my dad and mom were in front. They saw the grimace of pain on my face. They also knew I wouldn't return so soon unless something was wrong.

Dad took me to the emergency room, and when the doctor heard the story, he was incredulous that I had survived the fall. After taking X-rays and finding no broken bones, the doctor said, "You should have broken your back by landing on your feet like that, or you should have been killed."

The impact on my feet was so intense that, when I landed, one smooth river rock had pushed through the boot sole and created a huge bruise to the bone and a large, round blood blister, without breaking through the shoe's sole. Because of the injuries to my feet and legs, I had to crawl around the house for a week before I could put weight on my feet.

Every so often, the unanswered questions haunt me. Was it an angelic voice that spoke to my spirit, telling me to stand up? Were the two male angels sent specifically to help me?

I look back at that experience with the realization that God is a loving heavenly Father Who cares and watches over His children. I was important enough to God that He was willing to spare my life by sending heavenly messengers to save me. This has given me a desire to share with others what God has done for me.

CHAPTER TWENTY-ONE

My Guardian Angel

Edwina Perkins

Cleaning one day, I discovered a note that had been hidden for two decades. Reading it helped me understand the struggles and fears of a young girl. Those words opened my eyes to see how close I'd come to death.

Cross-legged on our living room floor, I emptied the bottom shelf of the bookcase. A thin layer of dust, like fine gray hairs, puffed into the air. Condensed *Reader's Digests* were stacked to my right. I tossed into the giveaway box copies of *Dick and Jane* beginner readers and other assorted hardbacks.

I wiped my cleaning cloth across the sandpaperlike surface, erasing the outlines of my books, removing twenty-plus years of filth. As I worked, visible brush strokes appeared—aged white paint sparsely covered the bare wood—evidence of a hurried paint job.

I shook the cloth over the carpet. Dust bunnies flew. I refolded the damp rag and pushed it into the corner, almost crushing what lay hidden there.

I pulled out the yellowed note that had been creased in thirds, and then halved. I rubbed it across my jeans to remove the grime. The jagged edges of the notebook paper broke free as I opened the letter.

Dear Mother,

I recognized the flowing script. The strong slant to the right, the large letters. Janice's writing was easy for me to identify. Until her death when I was fourteen, I'd occasionally received cards from her, but nothing more. How I'd wanted much more.

Being out on my own has not been easy . . .

At nineteen and after her freshman year of college, Janice wanted to work in New York as a nanny. Several of her college friends were doing the same to earn money for their school year. For young, African American females in the South, jobs were scarce, so her parents allowed her to go. She didn't return to start her sophomore year.

I've made a mistake . . .

Janice had never lived in a big city before. An only child from a small town, she befriended another young girl—also a nanny—who taught her how to have a good time. Seven months after moving to Manhattan, she was alone, scared, and pregnant.

I don't know what to do . . .

The same friend suggested a solution to her problem. "No one will ever know," the friend said. "It won't take long. You'll be back to work the next day."

At nineteen, and believing she didn't have other options, she accepted the address scribbled on a scrap of a brown grocery bag, and shoved it into her purse. Several days later, she told her employer she needed to see a doctor. In her eyes, it wasn't a total lie.

That morning, she set out early for the subway. Noxious smells assaulted her the moment she descended the stairs. Cigarette smoke. Body odors. Pungent colognes and overpowering perfumes. She covered her nose with her coat collar; her stomach lurched, threatening to reject her small breakfast. Two stops later she hurried out of the subway and inhaled the cool air. But the nausea remained.

She rushed into the closest public bathroom and slammed the stall door. Her stomach emptied.

"Are you okay?" A stranger called from the other side of the door.

"Yeah." She gagged again. "No." Sweat beaded at her hairline.

She exited the stall. Splashed water on her face and rinsed her mouth, trying to ignore the stranger who watched.

"Are you sick?" the woman asked.

The kindness in the woman's voice and the concern in her eyes were too much. Janice burst into tears and shared what she was about to do.

"Please, don't," the woman said softly. "You don't know what this child could mean to you one day. There *is* another option."

The stranger gave her the name of a home for unwed mothers. "There's someone out there who will love your child."

She returned to the subway and headed home, willing to carry her pregnancy to term. And then give her baby away.

I need your help.

Complications threatened during her last month. With no health insurance or prenatal care, her employer suggested she contact her parents. "You're not our responsibility," they told her, "but we don't want anything to happen to you or the baby."

Can I come home?

I placed the letter in my lap, thinking how closely my life resembled hers. I was the same age she was when she wrote the letter. Dangling between my freshman and sophomore years, struggling with whether to return to school. Like her, I'd chosen to attend a college far from home. Would I make the same choices?

Janice's mother traveled north to bring her home. During the long car ride back to the South, she told her mother everything.

And she did find someone to love *both* of her children. Surprising everyone, she gave birth to twins. I was one of those twins.

My brother and I were adopted by our grandparents.

✦ ✦ ✦ ✦ ✦

I never thought my mother loved me. So many of my unanswered questions still remain just that–unanswered. But after reading the letter, I understood that she did love me in her own way. She loved me enough to give me life and a chance to have a family.

And I remembered the first time my grandmother told me the story.

"Who was the woman in the bathroom?" I asked.

She smiled. "Your guardian angel."

I folded the letter, tucked it in my back pocket, and tucked my mother back in my heart.

That woman was my guardian angel. Without her intervention, I wouldn't be here today.

Thank You, God, for sending Your angels to those who are hurt and confused.

CHAPTER TWENTY-TWO

Angel on Assignment

Renae Tolbert

What a long night, I thought as I walked to the employee parking lot behind Denny's where I worked. My feet hurt, I was tired, and the incident with Bob lingered in my mind.

It was a cold night in January, and I had a thirty-mile drive home to Denver. I didn't like working in Boulder, but I was in the restaurant business and wanted to climb the corporate ladder, so I went where they sent me. Besides, I had recently been divorced and had made the crazy decision to give custody of my three-year-old son to my ex-husband. I had no emotional support from my family so I worked a lot. When I worked, I felt needed. I loved my crew, and they valued me. We were a great team.

✦ ✦ ✦ ✦ ✦

I was thinking about Bob and really torn up about it. The incident seemed out of character for him. *A thief of all things, who would have thought?* My pondering brought to mind a string of hints and warnings that I probably should have noticed, but I didn't get them— only in retrospect.

Bob came into Denny's around eight o'clock every night, dressed in a yellow V-neck sweater stretched tightly over a collared white shirt, khaki slacks, and white tennis shoes. He carried a brief case and rode a bicycle. The top of his round head was bald but he had a blond ring of hair that extended around the back. I thought of him as a soft-looking man, quiet and polite.

Other than that, he stayed there the entire night, drinking coffee and rarely ordering a meal. Boulder is a college town, and we had lots of people who stayed all night with their noses in a book. No books, but Bob had his nose in his briefcase full of papers. He said he owned a car-cleaning place in town.

One of the waitresses came up to me. "I think you ought to know something." She nodded toward Bob. "He's lifting tips off the tables when he walks to the restroom."

"Are you sure?" I was so shocked I didn't know what else to say.

She told me she saw him swipe a tip from the edge of a table.

So we set him up. The next time he made his way to the men's room, his hand slipped from his pocket as he walked past a dollar bill on the edge of the table. The tip disappeared, and his hand slipped back into his pocket.

When I confronted him, he didn't try to defend himself, not even one word. He said, "Okay, no problem." He shuffled the papers back into his briefcase, walked out the door, got on his bike, and rode off into the cold, dark night.

We just never know, do we? Trying to put those thoughts to rest and go home for the night, I let out a heavy sigh, started the car, and flipped on the heater. Boulder, Colorado, is a cold place in January.

Just then, I looked up and saw Bob come out from behind the bushes. Instinct told me to lock the doors. I punched the lock down on my side and reached over and locked the passenger door. *Had he been hiding in the bushes waiting for me?*

I was scared, but since I knew him, I didn't feel the need to flee, and the doors were locked so I felt safe enough to let him talk to me through the window. But he didn't come to the window.

Without hesitation, he ran straight to the hatchback and climbed inside and into the backseat. Evidently, he was aware that the hatch on a Volkswagen Rabbit had to be locked manually. Unfortunately, I had forgotten to lock it.

He leaned over my right shoulder. Yanking the keys from the ignition, he growled, "Move over, I'm driving." I had an amazing amount of calm and courage that must have come from the Lord. I wouldn't budge, nor did I scream.

"What are you doing?"

He pulled me down toward the passenger seat and put his gloved hand around my neck. My feline instincts kicked in and I began scratching his face. He grabbed my right hand and held it firmly against my throat, the keys pressed into my windpipe. I continued struggling to scratch his face and eyes with my left hand. He finally got both my hands trapped under his grip, but that meant he wasn't able to do anything else because if he let go, I would claw at his face.

I didn't think anyone would hear me scream so I kept kicking, hoping he would give up and leave. At one point, I used my foot to unlock the driver door. He let go of my hand to lock it again. That gave me an opportunity to claw him.

At last, I heard people walking by the car.

"Help! Help, get me out!" I screamed.

He shoved the cold keys into my mouth and I bit his finger through his glove. I tasted blood. He became enraged and distracted by the pain from my bite. I clawed his face again. Blood rolled from his face like tears, dripping onto my face and jacket. Then with my hand still free, I reached behind my head and unlocked the passenger door.

My car door opened and two strong hands wedged their way under my arms and gently placed me on the ground.

Bob climbed out the back of my Volkswagen and took off running with my keys in his hand. I stood up and ran after him, raising my fist and screaming angry words into the darkness. When I realized the person who pulled me out of the car wasn't running after him with me, I stopped at the edge of the cold, dark parking lot, exhausted and emotionally distraught.

I turned to thank the man who rescued me, only to realize he was gone. He couldn't have run away that quickly. But he was gone. He had faded off into the cold, frosty air of the night.

The police will never believe me when I tell them an angel pulled me out of the car. I would have no witnesses or evidence to this crime other than the blood and bruises on my neck. That would have to be enough. And it was.

That happened thirty years ago.

I will never know who my angel was, but I thank God for sending him on that cold, dark night. He was not only sent by God, but that mugging catapulted me into making life-changing decisions. Two months later I moved fourteen hundred miles away, started on a new path, and got my life together. Ultimately, I got my son back. We both became believers, and I met my soulmate.

Although I didn't know the Lord intimately at that time, He protected me by sending an angel. God also gave me strength to leave Denver and start a new life in California.

CHAPTER TWENTY-THREE

Out of the Depths

Sandy Adams

Mama had one of her "bad feelings" about the party and didn't want me to go. "But it's Christy's birthday," I begged. "I have to go."

Christy and I had been friends since second grade. How could I possibly miss her twelfth birthday party and still remain best friends forever? The fact that it was a swim party at the river and I didn't know how to swim was immaterial. I couldn't miss that party or my social life would be over.

After a few hours of near-hysteria on my part, Mama conceded. When I told Christy, she was as thrilled as I was. To celebrate our victory, she persuaded her mom to buy both of us new swimsuits for the special occasion. We wanted to look totally fabulous for the inaugural boys-included birthday extravaganza.

The day of the exhilarating event was sunny and warm. A good omen, we decided. "Everything is going to be perfect," I said.

Then I looked in the mirror and there it was—a giant zit. Mama's bad feelings were right. How could I appear in public with that thing? As a typical twelve-year-old, I could only wail, "My life is over."

Despite her foreboding, Mom rushed to the drugstore to buy a waterproof acne cover-up. With the makeup and wearing my new swimsuit, I was once again sure to be the hit of the party, second to Christy, of course. After all, this was her special day.

The party was everything I dreamed it would be. Including boys. They certainly changed the atmosphere of a party. We had entered a new level of entertainment. Christy and I felt we were on top of the world. To make it even more fun, there were plenty of rafts and inner tubes to go around, so I thought, *Who needs to know how to swim anyway?* My secret was as covered as the zit under all that concealer, and the equipment meant I didn't have to show I couldn't swim.

Shortly after lunch, as I floated lazily on a pink raft, one of the boys decided it would be funny to flip my raft and dump me into the water. Before I could grab the raft for safety, he swam out of my reach with it. He didn't know that I couldn't swim.

I surfaced long enough to see him climb aboard my beautiful pink lifesaver, laughing with his buddies as they paddled across the river.

Mama's words came back to remind me that she had had a bad feeling. Why did she have to be right? I thought of the fear in her eyes, and I began to panic. *Why hadn't I listened to her? Why had I insisted on having my way?*

I kicked as hard as I could, but the water felt thick and my legs were weak. I surfaced again, reaching for anything to lift me from what I feared was my soon-to-be watery grave. I raised my hands high, struggling to find something to pull myself up on, but there was nothing. I willed my tired legs to kick harder, only to realize that I had sunk to my ankles into the river's muddy bottom.

I knew then. It was over.

I'd heard that when we're about to die, we see our life pass before us. At the age of twelve, unfortunately, there was not much to review, but what there had been, I saw. I was surprised by the strange things my mind chose to remember. Everyday events, seemingly unimportant at the time, flashed before me like long-forgotten treasures, dusted and polished for inspection.

I also saw my obituary. My brother had moved into my bedroom. Sadly, I saw Mama weeping uncontrollably because she had given in to my willfulness. I ached for her as I sensed her feelings of being responsible for her daughter's death. I hadn't ever imagined such painful emotions.

I could no longer hold my breath, my lungs burned for lack of air. The last thing I remember was the taste of mud as I inhaled, and the turbid river water entering my mouth.

I awoke on the pier coughing and struggling to maintain that precious gift of life, which I had come so close to losing. Through blurry eyes, I saw a crowd gathered around me. Everyone was speaking at once. I was confused and crying, and yet I felt unexpected peace and comfort as a man's hand stroked my face. He was wet from head to toe, wearing shiny black shoes, dark slacks, and a white shirt. Before I could look at his face, Christy's mom grabbed me and began lecturing me about what a foolish thing I had done.

I didn't know which foolish thing I had done and couldn't concentrate. Just then, and probably still in shock, I screamed with all my might, "Who saved me?"

Someone said, "He did," pointing in the direction of a man walking away wearing the clothes I had seen when he gently stroked my face. I struggled to stand on weak, shaky legs. I wanted to go to him and thank him for saving my life. However, by the time I got to my feet and turned in his direction, he was gone. Vanished.

Everyone was as surprised as I was to see that the sidewalk leading to the parking lot held wet footprints stopping in midstride. The man was gone and no one saw where he went.

A hush came over the frantic crowd. There was no explanation for his sudden disappearance in such a large, open area. I was as certain then as I am now that God had sent one of His angels to rescue me. No one will ever convince me otherwise.

My life changed that day. For the first time, I knew that I mattered. I believed that the future held promise and opportunities I had never before imagined. In a sense, I did die that day. I died to my old way of thinking that my life didn't matter or that no one really cared. It does matter—every life matters.

Many years have passed since that life-changing visitation, but its effect hasn't diminished. Since then, it's become my passion to help others see the value and purpose in their lives. I have been blessed with the opportunity to encourage thousands of people by teaching at seminars and conferences, helping them to recognize their own self-worth. God created each of us with a purpose and He cares about all of us.

I'm thankful that God sent one of His faithful servants to save a seemingly insignificant twelve-year-old girl that day. For out of the insignificant comes the extraordinary. I'll be forever grateful to the angel who turned a river of death into my river of life. And to the one true God Who lifted me out of the depths of an ordinary life into an extraordinary depth of understanding about my own worth and value.

CHAPTER TWENTY-FOUR

Roadside Guardian

JoAnn Reno Wray

In 1975, we took a summer trip from our Ohio home to North Carolina. As we drove the last leg toward home, darkness closed in. After hours on the road, we were exhausted.

Five-year-old Amie sprawled on the backseat, sleeping with one hand across her eyes. Mike, three years old, snuggled with his blanket on the carpeted floor. That was long before seat belts were required.

Roger stretched one arm over his head. "I need a break," he said. "Watch for a rest area. There should be one coming up soon."

I repositioned myself and leaned forward. "I could use a break too. I'm glad we're stopping."

Before long we spotted the sign announcing a rest area with facilities one mile ahead. Roger pulled in and turned off the engine. The silence felt like wool in my ears after hours of road noise. No other cars or people were about. In the soft summer night, crickets accompanied a mockingbird's melody.

Completely without concern, not for one second considering our children's safety, we made sure they still slept, and hurried to the restroom. I spent five minutes inside and Roger even less. When I came out, he was marching up and down the sidewalk, stopping occasionally to do jumping jacks. I stretched my arms and touched my toes a few times. We both grabbed a drink of cold water from the fountain and splashed some on our faces.

"Ready to go?" Roger wanted to get home before midnight and it was 10:45 PM already.

"Should we make the kids go potty or just let them sleep?" I asked.

"Let them sleep. They're fine. If they need to stop, I'll find a place."

We got into the car, never checking the backseat, and soon zoomed along the highway with the wind whistling through the windows. I dozed off. When I woke, the dashboard clock glowed 11:25 PM.

I twisted around in my seat to check the kids.

"The backseat is empty!" I screamed. I stretched over the seat where Mike slept soundly. Amie's gone!" A fearful panic engulfed me. "Roger, Amie's gone!"

"Gone? How–"

Sobbing and screaming, I grabbed his shoulder, shaking him.

"Are you sure?" Roger's eyebrows rose in alarm as his forehead furrowed.

"She's not there. Stop the car!" Roger pulled on to the berm and slammed on the brakes. We both jumped out and flung open the back doors.

Amie was gone.

Mike still slept undisturbed. I bent down and shook him gently, "Mike, honey, wake up."

He sat up, confused, his thumb in his mouth.

"Where's Amie? Do you know?"

Out came the thumb. "On the swings."

"What swings?"

"Where we stopped." He rubbed his eyes. "Sleep now?"

I trembled, but tried to stay calm. "Yes, sleep." I patted his back a few seconds, then softly closed the doors.

Before we climbed back in the car, hysteria raged, and I couldn't control my emotions. "She's at the rest area. She's all alone. Someone might take her or worse. We have to go now."

Roger had already figured that out and nodded. Although outwardly calm, inside he was probably as upset as I was.

Despite signs forbidding such a maneuver, Roger whipped a U-turn. He calmly said, "We've probably traveled almost forty miles since our stop." The only sign of his concern was that he exceeded the speed limit and the set of his face showed he wouldn't let anything stop us from reaching the rest area as quickly as possible.

"Please protect her, God. Keep her safe." My heart beat wildly while my feet pressed into the floor trying to make the car go faster. Internally, I yelled at myself for being such a bad parent and asked God for forgiveness.

Roger's face was icy white, his forehead beaded with sweat, as his hands clamped like iron on the steering wheel.

We finally pulled into the parking lot of the dimly lit rest area. This time there were three or four other cars.

"Please, let her be there. Let her be there."

I saw the three cars and several people, but my eyes targeted our precious daughter.

"There she is," I yelled. Her blonde curls bobbed as she skipped down the sidewalk.

The car brakes squealed and both of us hurried out of the car. Roger passed me, grabbed Amie, and hugged. My arms surrounded them both as we huddled on the sidewalk. I wept in relief and so did Roger.

Amie squirmed. "You're squeezing me. Let me down."

I laughed at the normalcy of her response.

Roger put her down. Frustration and relief combined as he shouted, "Amie, why did you get out of the car? We've told you not to do that without us."

"I wanted to play on the swings," she said, completely unconcerned.

"But it was dark and—"

"You took too long." She tilted her head and smiled innocently. "The man in the sparkly clothes said you were coming back." She pointed to the dark playground behind the restrooms. "That man. He's right there."

Roger and I turned, but neither of us saw anyone.

Amie's eyes widened, her mouth forming an open pink circle of surprise. She giggled. "He waved at me, but he's gone now. He myst-a-peered."

Goose bumps raced down my spine. I put my hand on Amie's shoulder to reassure myself she was really there. Roger's head whipped back and forth, peering into the darkness. No one stood or sat where Amie pointed.

Even though it was nearly midnight, people sat at tables with snacks and soft drinks, and kids shouted and played. We learned that the cars belonged to a family group, caravanning cross-country. Roger and I approached them and asked if anyone had seen the man Amie described.

They looked puzzled and said no or shook their heads.

As we walked back to the car, I kept saying to Roger and to our daughter, "No one had seen him. How could that be?"

I squatted down to eye-level with Amie. "Are you sure you saw the man with the sparkly clothes?"

"Yes, Mommy. He pushed me on the swings and he stayed with me while you were gone." She laughed and said, "And he was a nice man."

I stood up and took Roger's hand as Amie bounced down the sidewalk ahead of us and climbed into the backseat of our car. Roger and I leaned our foreheads together.

"Thank You, God. Thank You, God, that she's safe." Roger could barely choke out the words.

"Yes. Thank You, God," I echoed.

We had failed as perfect parents, been neglectful, and driven off leaving Amie in the dark of night at a place far from home. What happened that day stopped any casual approach to parenting we'd had.

God had given us a second chance by sending a roadside guardian in sparkly clothing to protect our little girl.

CHAPTER TWENTY-FIVE

Through Angel Eyes

Elizabeth Baker

I lived with ugly for a long time and it had become invisible. Trash is normal. Unwashed dishes are something I should take care of, and I would. Later. The laundry piled in corners didn't matter because those clothes were out of season anyway. We bought our sofa at a garage sale, and it was a little shabby then. Why should I bother dusting tables or removing the blankets from the floor?

There can be many reasons for a young family to live in filth. None of them are good. For me, it was a combination of depression and revenge against my husband for not making my dreams come true. I had a long list of grievances against him, not the least of which was his refusal to go to church with the baby and me.

When I left the house one Sunday morning, the baby and I looked fine. We were clean, brushed, and smiling; no one knew the chaos we lived in at home. I liked to attend church, but week after week of watching those happy families only deepened my depression.

Rather than responding to the sermons with repentance, resentment built up inside me. I didn't want to be in this awful place. It was all Bill's fault. Why did he have to rent a farm house for us rather than something in town? The country might have been his dream, but it wasn't mine.

When the service was over, I drove down tree-lined roads and back to the ugly house. When I pulled in the gravel drive I expected to see Bill somewhere around the barn. He usually waved or came out to the car, but I didn't see him anywhere.

I opened the back door and kicked stray shoes out of the way. "Bill?" I called.

There was no answer.

Voices came from the living room. I put my sleeping baby down and continued to listen. The voices definitely weren't the TV. A middle-aged woman sat on the sofa with a girl about six years old on one side and a boy of maybe ten on the other. She looked up and smiled. "Did you enjoy church?"

I felt too stunned to reply.

"Your husband invited us in," she said. She didn't look threatening, but something about the little group made my skin prickle. We hadn't had company in the house since we moved in two years earlier.

"Our car broke down and your husband–isn't his name Bill?" She looked to her son who solemnly nodded. "Yes, I've got it right." She continued as though the boy had given her a good grade on a test. "Bill let us in and said you would be back from church soon. He and John are working on the car."

"*Uhhh*, I'm glad he could help."

"I folded the towels for you," she said and smiled. "I moved them from the sofa. Hope you don't mind."

There had been laundry on the couch? I looked absentmindedly around the room. What happened to the blanket that was on the floor in front of the television? I had no idea what to say or do next. Exactly what should I do with company? I had almost forgotten what it was like to have anyone visit.

"Could I get you some water," I said to cover up my uncertainty, "or something?" My voice sounded tense. I took a breath and tried to relax.

"That would be nice. Thank you very much."

Back in the kitchen, there were no clean glasses. In fact, I wasn't sure we owned glasses anymore. For the last couple of months we drank from old canning jars. If we still owned drinking glasses, they would be on the top shelf. I pulled over a chair, climbed up, and reached. I sighed in relief. My fingers felt four glasses, pushed onto the back of the shelf. I pulled them into the light, and they were dusty.

I jumped down and looked around the kitchen for a towel. Nothing. That must have been one of the things I had left piled on the sofa. *Oh well*, I thought, *the end of my full skirt makes a good substitute*.

As I dusted the glasses and filled them, I kept thinking about the woman and those two children. Something about them unnerved me. She seemed unnaturally relaxed and friendly. Perhaps that's what it was. I had been so lonely and miserable, I didn't know what a contented face looked like.

Her face seemed to radiate good will and acceptance. She acted as though she dropped into strangers' homes every day—dirty, filthy homes like ours. But I had detected no judgmentalism, no unkindness.

Just then, a verse from the Bible (Hebrews 13:2) came to mind that we should be careful to entertain strangers because by doing so some people had entertained angels unaware. *Angels? How could they be angels? Kids can't be angels, can they? Do angels get thirsty? They looked so–so ordinary*.

"And so happy," I said out loud.

I filled four glasses but because I had no tray to carry them on, I pressed them together as I had once seen a waitress do and carefully balanced them as I carried them into the living room.

"I didn't get your name." She smiled and said, "I'm Carol."

"Most people call me Judy," I said, "but I like Elizabeth better. That's on my birth certificate."

"Elizabeth, I am very glad to know you. Did you plant those roses by the front steps?"

There were roses by the front steps? I knew we had front steps, but I'd never bothered to investigate. No one ever entered through the front door anyway, and the steps only led to an ancient porch with loose boards and rusted screens curling at the edges.

Before I could think of a response, she said, "They are only in bud stage, but I think they will be bright red, and they've climbed nearly to the roofline." She smiled again and added, "I'm sure you must enjoy looking at them."

I smiled but said nothing.

For the next hour, Carol did most of the talking while I sat quietly. I was enthralled by her voice and cheery disposition. Her two children said nothing, only sipped their water and followed the adult conversation with animated eyes.

Carol pointed out the beautiful and the possible. Had I ever noticed the intricate grain in the wood-paneled walls? Wasn't spring wonderful this year? The sunshine was warm and if the drapes were opened a little it would fill the room. Bluebonnets bloomed all along the roadside. Wouldn't they make a delightful bouquet?

She didn't condemn me or suggest I pay more attention to my home. Rather, she described what she saw when she looked at my familiar surroundings with eyes focused on the pleasing and the lovely.

What kind of woman was she? I felt such acceptance by her and wondered how she could see such dirt and lack of care and yet point out the beauty.

About that time both men entered the house. Bill led the way to the front door—the one with the rosebush ready to bloom. He pulled open the rusty screen and told our guest to watch his step on the loose boards.

"The car's running smoothly," Carol's husband said. "Bill did a fine job."

Carol collected the glasses and set them on the end table while the children shook my hand like miniature adults. They thanked us again and left.

I felt sad as the car disappeared and I turned back to the house with a sigh. I scrutinized the room and tried to see it as Carol did. She had folded the blanket I had missed earlier and placed it neatly at the end of the sofa below an end table. Why hadn't I thought of that before? It certainly looked better folded there than crumpled in the middle of the floor.

I walked into the kitchen. Garbage, trash, and scattered clothing assaulted me. Depression started to take over. *It's filthy*, I thought, *but it's just too much work*. Too much to do–too much. I decided to flop on the sofa and watch television.

Just then a bird began to sing. It was just an ordinary chickadee and the chirping wasn't particularly melodic. Yet like Carol's words, it drew me to something pleasant within my chaotic surroundings. I paused and looked around. If I opened the window, I might hear more. With a shove and a little pounding, the old wooden sash slowly lifted. Fragrant air joined the bird's warble.

Carol was right. It was indeed a lovely spring.

Slowly, one chore at a time, our home began to improve. I stopped looking at all I couldn't do and what I didn't have. Instead,

I focused on the possibilities that small differences could make. As my home environment cleared, so did my mind. I slept less, cried less, and began to peel away my self-pity one stubborn layer at a time.

I've always wondered about the visitors who came that Sunday afternoon. Were they angels? I'm not given to romantic thought or fantasy, but I've never been able to convince myself they weren't some kind of special angels fulfilling an assignment to lift me out of my depression and to help me appreciate life.

I know that in a single afternoon I briefly saw my world through different eyes—through angel eyes—and nothing has ever looked the same again.

CHAPTER TWENTY-SIX

Stranded in Russia

Sonya Lee Thompson

I can't believe we are actually doing this," I said to Tim, my husband. After nine months of grueling paperwork and meetings, we were in flight to Russia to adopt our baby girl Katia.

My stomach churned with excitement. I smiled. After months of longing for that little girl, we were finally going to meet her face to face. How would she look? What would she smell like? How would she react to us? Many, many questions raced through my mind on the fourteen-hour plane trip to Moscow.

I'd flown many times before, but not like this. It was May 2000, and we were on board a Russian airline. Cigarette smoke permeated the air.

A majority of the passengers spoke Russian, a language my husband and I never learned. We spoke a few basic words and phrases such as no, yes, and where's the bathroom?

It didn't matter. I reminded myself that an interpreter would meet us at the airport and guide us through everything we had to do.

Our plane finally landed at Moscow's Sheremetyevo International Airport. Although I'd flown many times, I'd never been out of the country before, and neither of us knew what to expect. Fear of the unknown and the anticipation of finally holding my new daughter almost became too much for me. I felt lightheaded, and my mouth went dry.

Gathering our hand luggage, we exited the plane onto the tarmac. "No fancy terminals in Moscow," I said to no one in particular. It looked as if we had been time warped back to the 1920s.

Once inside the airport, officials ushered everyone into one large room. I had been warned about this part of our journey—customs and immigration. We had to declare the amount of American money we carried. The Russian banks had failed, so American cash had become the accepted form of currency. We had been told we couldn't use traveler's checks or money orders either.

Fearing the worst, Tim and I decided to separate the fifteen thousand dollars in cash we had with us. After clearing customs and declaring how much money we brought into the country, we stuffed wads of cash onto our bodies. The worst part was there was only a clear Plexiglas wall separating us from others waiting to go through immigration. No privacy heightened my fear of being robbed.

From there, they escorted us to the luggage area to look for our bags. Nothing seemed to move quickly, but I didn't mind. I was in Russia. *Soon, soon,* I kept telling myself.

Can this really be happening? My thoughts focused on my soon-to-be new baby girl. Peace came over me; it was God's presence.

One by one, Tim pulled our bags off the conveyer belt. Planning to be in Russia for fourteen days meant several large bags of luggage. Excitedly, we moved toward the main lobby of the airport. It was surprisingly small but clean. We could easily see from one end to the other.

At first there had been a scurry of activity and many voices around us as people grabbed their luggage and headed for the exit doors to enter Moscow.

We looked for our interpreter, but she wasn't there. We waited for at least thirty minutes, and I silently fretted and paced. *Where is she? Has traffic delayed her? Surely she wouldn't just not show up, would she? What do we do if she doesn't come?*

A feeling of abandonment overcame me. Anxiety and fear rose from within. I was a stranger, my first time in a foreign country, and I didn't know the language. Tim was calm and seemed unperturbed, but I was an emotional mess and getting worse. I wanted to see my baby.

What happened to the earlier peace of God's presence? I wondered. Faith is believing that which isn't seen, I reminded myself.

Another ten minutes and everything quieted down and the airport cleared out except for cab drivers who still lined the exit doors to solicit customers.

"Honey, the food I ate on the plane is going right through me," Tim said. "I have to leave you here with our luggage and go to a restroom."

Despite my anxiety and not wanting him to leave me, I said nothing, and Tim rushed to the men's room.

I waited with the luggage as Tim walked out of sight. Time seemed to stand still as I impatiently waited for his return. My gaze frequently swept around the area, seeking our interpreter. We had been given her local number in case something like this occurred. I looked around. Where were the telephones? I couldn't see any booths and our cell phones were of no use in this country.

"Dear God," I prayed. "Please help us. We're stranded, and I'm scared. Lord, I don't speak their language. I don't know how to ask for help."

Just then, one of the cab drivers walked toward me. He looked different from the others, perhaps because he was taller than anyone else was. He must have been about six feet four with dark brown hair. He smiled at me with the most amazing sky blue eyes–that color was a rarity in that part of the world. He asked me something in Russian so I repeatedly said "Nyet" and tried to avoid eye contact.

Then he said, "Sprechen Sie Deutsch?" (Do you speak German?)

I assumed the cab drivers knew several phrases in different languages, but this man resonated with me. My dad took German in school and often spoke to us in that language. He used to drill us with simple phrases. As odd as it sounds, the cab driver's question caused me to have an unexplained inner peace and an inclination to trust him.

With no sign of Tim or our interpreter, I took a deep breath and said, "Not German. English. We're Americans."

"May I be of service to you?" he asked in only slightly accented English. I wondered how many cab drivers in Russia knew several languages fluently like that man. "I have seen you waiting here for a very long time."

I explained that our interpreter hadn't shown up. I pulled out the phone number we had for her. Feeling safe with him, I asked, "How do I make a phone call from the airport?"

"First, you will need rubles to make the phone call," he said. "Do you have any?"

I shook my head and explained that we had been told only to use American money.

"I will take care of it." He asked for cash and I felt no hesitation in trusting him. I gave him a ten-dollar bill to have it exchanged.

He smiled and walked down the corridor.

Shortly after he left, Tim returned. I explained what happened and that the nice cab driver was going to convert our money into Russian rubles. He laughed at me and said, "I'm glad it was only ten dollars because there's no way we'll ever see him again."

"You're probably right," I said. As I said those words, I rebuked myself for trusting my naïve instincts.

Much to our surprise, the driver returned. He handed me the rubles and an exchange slip that accounted for every penny.

Back home, someone had told me that ten American dollars was the equivalent of about two weeks' income to a cab driver. Honesty was yet another unusual trait for that mysterious man.

"I'll take you," he said. Without waiting for an answer, he picked up our two largest bags, and led us into a gated phone area in the airport. Inside the gates were several booths with archaic looking phones and one chair at each desk. He took the phone number from me and counted out a number of rubles from those I held. He took them and spoke to the woman attending the booths.

He came back and nodded toward the booths. "Use the phone at station three," he said. "You will have only five minutes to talk." He closed the gate and stood guard while Tim and I went to the booth.

I picked up the phone and made the call. I spoke hurriedly and nervously to the interpreter's husband who spoke English. He apologized and told us she had confused our arrival time. She had become aware of her mistake and was on her way.

Relieved, the three of us dragged our baggage back to the main lobby area of the airport to wait for her arrival. I leaned over and whispered to Tim, "I think he's my guardian angel."

Tim smiled and reached into his pocket to pull out a ten-dollar bill to give it as a tip. He turned around. "Where is he?"

The man was gone.

We both looked around, scanning the nearly vacant building, but he was nowhere in sight. Impossible. How could a six-foot-four man disappear in seconds from inside a nearly empty Russian airport?

Immediately we prayed and thanked God for taking such good care of us by sending my guardian angel in this great time of need.

Our interpreter showed up shortly afterward, and we went on to adopt our precious baby girl.

For the remainder of our trip, we were at peace. We had a few difficulties but they seemed insignificant. We knew—truly knew—we could trust God completely with our lives, even far away from home.

CHAPTER TWENTY-SEVEN

Subway Angel with a Sidekick

Patricia Lee

We stared at the New York City skyline the day my mother, a church friend, and I arrived. I gawked like the small-town girl I was, but I was determined not to let the metropolitan giant daunt my spirits.

Not yet out of college, and cocky by nature, I dubbed myself the tour guide for our band of three travelers. I studied the subway maps and read the handbook of tourist attractions. I made schedules as if I knew what I was doing. My mother and my friend let me do everything, and they followed me.

Midway through our visit, I planned a subway ride to what I thought of as the far edge of the city. As a college student from a small town, I viewed the ride to the museum to be long and complicated.

I noted the trains and their arrival times for both directions. I felt confident we would reach our appointed destination without difficulty. We had only to arrive on time, catch the train, get off, and transfer to the next one.

"We won't have any problems," I assured them and showed them my itinerary.

The following morning we left for the first leg of our journey. We got off the subway to catch a connecting train. Instead of seeing the train I counted on being there, we found a deserted subway platform with no one around.

The vacant platform filled me with an eerie sense of foreboding. We waited for several minutes in the semidark underground, but the station remained empty. None of the subway cars rumbling by bothered to stop.

My bravado faded. *What did I do wrong?* I kept asking myself. *How did I mess up like this?*

My mother and my friend studied the timetables posted around us, but none of us could figure out why no train stopped. I wondered how long we would be stuck here. My small-town girl brain conjured up all kinds of nasty endings. Had I brought my companions to a place of danger?

While we stood there pondering our next move, out of the darkness appeared a large and heavy-set black woman and her young son. I blinked, wondering what entrance she'd come through. The woman waddled on tired legs, her tent dress draped over her large frame. Glasses rested on her nose and perspiration beaded on her round face, but her eyes peered straight at me. The boy, about eight, simply stared at us.

I stood there, subway schedule in one hand, tour book in the other–the picture of the wayward tourist–wondering where I'd gone wrong.

The woman apparently sized up our situation. "Where you folks looking to go?"

I explained our destination was a historic house now open as a museum. I told her the hotel where we were staying and which train I thought we should ride. I pointed to the map. "Why aren't the trains stopping here?"

"It's the right station," she said, "but that route only runs mornings and evenings. You're going to have a long wait if you want that one."

I turned to my two companions to ask what we should do.

"Don't worry. Come on, I'll take you where you can get to your museum house."

I stared at my companions with a silent question. Should we trust her? What if we were being led to a bigger problem? Lacking any other option, I shrugged and said to my mother, "Let's go."

The woman led us up a set of stairs and to another platform where subway cars waited and urged us to get on.

I wondered where that train was bound. The unknown haunted me. We were on a train we didn't expect, riding under a city we didn't know, led by a woman we'd never met before. The whole predicament smelled of disaster.

The large woman got on the subway car and rode with us. In fact, she stayed with us the entire twenty minutes before leading us to a connecting route and changing trains with us again.

When she led us up and out of the subway, she pointed up the street. "Walk about five blocks and you'll find your house. Then come back to this station. You get on here going south, and without changing trains you'll be able to return to your hotel."

We nodded that we understood while she and the boy walked away. Instead of returning to the subway, they headed down the sidewalk away from us. I thought it strange that she wouldn't go back the way she'd come.

We stared up the street and read the street signs. Sure enough, we were on the street where we needed to be.

Realizing I hadn't thanked the woman or gotten her name, I spun around to thank her. I gawked at an empty street. The woman and the boy had disappeared. How could they have gotten away so quickly?

✦ ✦ ✦ ✦ ✦

I've thought about that woman many times in the years that followed our trip. Who was she? What would have happened to us if she hadn't come along?

The Bible contains many references to a realm of angels used in annunciations, ministering to Jesus, and freeing persons held in captivity. In recent times we read much about angels in our lives, from mysterious sightings to television programs proclaiming their existence.

On that day almost forty years ago in New York City, I believe God sent me an angel. She appeared in the form of a large, black woman sent to protect me from my own overconfidence.

One thing is certain. Of all the places I visited in New York City, whether they were houses, museums, or theaters, and of all the sights I saw as I blended with the tourist crowd, that woman remains the most vivid in my memory.

Even now, I often pause to thank God for her.

CHAPTER TWENTY-EIGHT

The Ski-Hill Angel

Wendy Toliver

I love where I live, with plenty of clean air and pristine scenery, including mountains, a lake, rivers, and wildlife. We can go to three ski resorts within ten minutes from our front door: Snowbasin, where the 2002 Olympics downhill events took place; the sprawling Powder Mountain Resort; and a locals' favorite, Wolf Mountain.

At sundown, we can enjoy the night skiing lights glowing from Wolf Mountain. That ski resort, with its four lifts, rickety barn-lodge, and affordable passes, is where my three boys learned to ski and snowboard. It's also where I learned to snowboard.

Every year with my grandma's Christmas money, my family buys season passes so we can drive up to Wolf Mountain on any winter morning, afternoon, or evening. As soon as snow falls, it becomes our home away from home.

January 30, 2014, was a crisp, blue-sky day of carefree mother-son adventure; definitely a day I thought would become one of my fondest memories. My four-year-old son Dawson and I rode the lift together.

As usual, he was regaling me with stories about what tricks he'd be doing on our next run. "I'm going to hit the box rail and then do that one jump by the pole–the really big one. Will you go first in case someone's in my way? It's going to be *so cool.*"

I was taking in the beautiful scenery when I realized Dawson had stopped talking. His bright yellow coat slid downward. I grabbed his mittened hand.

"Oh, God," I screamed. "Help me!" It was a desperate prayer, quite possibly the most desperate one I've ever uttered. I held on to his little hand with all my might as he dangled by one arm thirty feet above the hard, snow-packed ground. Sheer horror clamped its icy fingers around my heart.

Dawson stared up at me, big blue eyes wide with terror. As I anchored myself to the chair with one hand to keep from slipping off myself, I tried to put on a brave mom face for him. The chair swayed as his little legs kicked, trying futilely to propel himself back onto the chair. Gravity was playing a wicked game of tug of war with me, while ghastly visions of Dawson falling filled my mind.

I tried not to focus on the probability he would break bones and the possibility he could die. I knew the prospect of pulling his forty-pound body, weighed down further by skis and boots, back up into the safety of the chair seemed impossible.

I have a circulation disease called Raynaud's, and at that time I had no feeling in my hands. His mitten was slipping out of my grip, and despite my efforts, my youngest son was dropping. I've never felt so hopeless. I realized the impossibility of this Herculean task.

I cannot give up on my little boy. God, God, please . . .

If I jumped off the chair, could I make it to the ground first and pad his fall with my own body? I was heavier than he was. I also wondered if I should jump off or ride the lift the rest of the way up if or when he did fall. And if I could, by some stroke of luck, keep hold of him until we reached the top, what could the lift operator do to help? Are they even trained at this small ski resort to take care of emergency situations like this?

"Please, God, don't let me drop my baby!"

A voice called out, "Slowly. Steadily. Inch by inch."

I didn't look around to see who spoke to me. I squeezed Dawson's hand and pulled him up about an inch. My son gazed up at me. His beautiful blue eyes were no longer terror-stricken. Something much calmer resonated in them, a confidence that seemed to say, "You've got this, Mom. No sweat."

Filled with new-found determination, love, and the knowledge that my son believed in me, I took a deep breath and lifted him yet another inch.

"Slowly. Steadily. Inch by inch," the soothing voice repeated.

Finally, with only about fifty feet to go until we reached the top of the mountain, I pulled Dawson up to the safety of the chair.

I held Dawson tightly, squeezing his body against mine with all my lasting strength, careful not to let him see traces of fear or disbelief in my face. "Dear God, thank You," I whispered against his shiny blue helmet. I paused and stared downward, into that bright white oblivion that almost swallowed my son. But he was safe now. Both of us were.

We made it to the top of Wolf Mountain and got off the lift. Surprisingly, Dawson seemed to be fine. He merrily arranged his skis in launch position and without hesitation, took off down the hill toward the box rail he'd been talking about.

I couldn't keep my knees from wobbling. As I watched my little boy speeding down the hill, my entire body shook violently and uncontrollably, the way it feels after surgery when the anesthesia wears off. I wanted to fall to my knees the instant my snowboard touched the snowy ground, but I had to clear the way for whoever would be getting off next.

One of my girlfriends had been in a ski chair behind us. She thought maybe Dawson had fallen asleep, and that was why he'd slipped off. She could not believe I had the superhuman strength to pull him up. "I didn't," I said with a small smile. "An angel helped me."

She nodded, and I knew she believed me.

Later, Dawson told the rest of the family about the day's adventure. "At first, it was like, 'Whoa, this is scary.' Then it was like,

'Whoa, this is fun.'" Everyone chuckled at his rendition of the story and patted him on his back.

When my husband said, "Thank You, Lord, for saving our son," I shed my first tears.

That night on Facebook, I had upward of thirty comments voicing concern, relief, and awe. But each time someone mentioned my being a supermom–which may be how they saw me–I knew differently.

God sent an angel to whisper calming instructions and save my baby.

CHAPTER TWENTY-NINE

The Angel Visitation

Cathy Taylor with Nancy Aguilar

I lay perfectly still on the hospital scanning machine table with my arms and legs strapped down. Heaviness surrounded my heart like a shroud, but I purposely didn't cry because I couldn't wipe away the tears. My doctor had ordered a thyrogen scan to detect thyroid cancer. As I waited for it to begin, many questions raced through my mind: Did the radioactive iodine treatment work? Had the cancer reappeared and spread? Would I need surgery?

After twenty-three years in remission, my bloodwork had shown a possible recurrence of thyroid cancer. Over the next year and a half, I endured numerous medical procedures, tests, injections, and special diets.

During the ordeal, other members of my family experienced health issues as well. My mom received the diagnosis of recurrent lymphoma. My older brother Brian underwent chemotherapy, also for lymphoma. Most heartbreaking of all, my twin brother David became ill and died of the HIV virus.

The burden of afflictions in my family felt unbearable. Lying there on the table, I began praying the words from Isaiah 53:4 (ESV): "Surely He has borne our griefs and carried our sorrows."

As I finished praying those words, the atmosphere of the room changed. I can't explain it except to say I was in the presence of two angel-like beings. One stood tall on my left with arms folded across his chest, as if he was guarding me. The other stood very close on my right.

"What are you doing here?"

"We've come to comfort you," the angel on my right said.

"That's so nice," I said. As incredible as that may sound, my anxieties left, and I felt deep peace.

"We've come to dry your tears, just as you dried your brother's tears when he was dying." The angel on my right reached over and touched my cheek, as a father would do for his crying child.

"I'm not crying," I said.

"Your soul is crying."

"Yes, it is."

"Just as you once ministered to your brother David," the angelic being said, "now it's time to minister to your mother."

I knew exactly what the angel meant. "Yes, I'll do that," I said.

"Your scan will be clear and you will be made well," the being on my right said.

As suddenly as the angels had appeared, they left. Then my tears began to fall and roll down the side of my face. I couldn't wipe them away, and that was all right because they were tears of joy.

What I had seen were strong, malelike figures with light shining from behind and around them. They resembled holograms and were the color of pewterlike flowing mercury. Ezekiel 8:2 (ESV) describes heavenly beings as having ". . . the appearance of a man. Below what appeared to be his waist was fire, and above his waist was something like the appearance of brightness, like gleaming metal."

When the scan was over, I walked out of the room and into my doctor's office, grinning. I had gone from deep despair to pure joy. The doctor told me that even though my scan was clear, "You'll have to wait for the results of your final blood test." (His nurse had earlier drawn the blood.)

I told my family and a few friends about the angels' visitation. "I don't know what it all means," I said, "but I know I'm going to be all right."

The following week, I received the news that my blood tests showed thyroid cancer "somewhere," and my doctor ordered a PET scan to determine if I needed surgery. I cried and cried, asking the Lord to help me understand.

"Trust me." I didn't hear those words out loud, but they echoed through my heart and gave me peace. I completed the scan and felt confident that the Lord would bring healing; however, I assumed that I'd have to go through much suffering to be made well.

As I waited for the results, pondering all that had happened, I realized the angels had visited me *after* the nurse had taken my blood. Once more, I felt hopeful, wondering if I had been healed after the blood tests were done.

Lord, please let it be true.

The next week, I woke up on Tuesday morning and a voice within said these words to me, "Before you hear the news from your doctor. I want you to rejoice that you're healed."

With renewed joy in my heart, I spent a delightful day at the zoo with my son Nick. That evening at 7:30, my doctor called me at home. I was visibly shaking and burst out with the question, "Is it good news or bad news?"

"I've been poring over your PET scan results," he said, "and I can't find cancer cells anywhere in your body. According to your blood work, we should have found something, but you are totally clear."

"Do you think it's possible that I was healed sometime between my bloodwork and my thyrogen scan?"

"It's certainly a possibility," he said. He talked for several minutes before he finished with these wonderful words: "I don't need to see you for a year. No surgery. No more radiation–just relax and have a good summer."

Today, six years later, my follow-up exams continue to show no cancer. My fear of death is gone. I'm assured that when it's time, God will send angels to escort me home.

God has been so gracious to me, and I am humbled by His mercy. The Lord did it all, and God always does all things well.

CHAPTER THIRTY

The Messenger

Debbie Johnson with Gloria Ashby

Your father-in-law's condition is grave, Mrs. Johnson," the physician said. "Tests show he has suffered several small strokes and has a weakened heart. I wish I had better news, but the prognosis doesn't look good."

He paused as if he were studying the shine on his shoes, but I believe he wanted to avoid the pleading in my eyes. I imagined he had seen my look on the faces of other families–the look that searched for a hope he couldn't give.

Leaning against the wall for support, I struggled for control. Tears threatened to spill from my eyes. "There's nothing more you can do?"

"We can only pray and keep him comfortable." While fumbling with a button on his starched white lab coat, the doctor stared at some unseen spot on the wall behind me and continued to avoid looking at me. "I'm so sorry." He turned and walked silently toward the ICU exit, leaving me alone to absorb his words.

Swiping at the tears that now trailed down my cheeks, I wondered how to tell my husband and his family. *Why me? Why had I volunteered to corner the doctor this morning? Why are Johnny and his brother out of town? They should be the ones here with their father. His sister Ann should be here. Not me.* My thoughts raced. How can I tell my mother-in-law that he's dying?

Dear God, I didn't expect this. I don't want to do this.

I looked through the doorway at my father-in-law, unmoving beneath the pristine white sheet. Tubes and tangled monitor wires seemed to poke out from every orifice of his body. Closing my eyes, I wished I could be transported to a different place—anywhere but here.

Was it only last night when we left his room encouraged by his pinker skin tone and stronger voice? Was it less than twenty-four hours ago when we left his bedside clinging to hope? Hope that he'd rally.

I opened my eyes and sighed, still standing in the hospital corridor. A nurse passed me with a breakfast tray for the patient next door. Another wheeled an oxygen tank to a room across the hallway. The hushed voices of doctors dictating patient histories and of two nurses working together to stock a medication cart floated from the nurses' station as shifts changed and the day came to life.

The day came to life everywhere, that is, except in my father-in-law's room. He lay motionless with only the rhythmic beep of his heart monitor testifying he was alive.

I turned to leave, my shoulders slumped under the burden of truth I had heard. *My father-in-law is dying.* And I had to be the one to tell the family. Wrapped in thought, I breathed deeply to control more tears threatening to spill from my eyes.

I hardly remembered pushing the down button or stepping into the empty elevator. The door opened to the lobby. I moved into the hospital's main entrance and trudged toward the door.

Warm rays of sun streamed through windows and brightened the lobby. Three steps away from the revolving door, a slightly built man with silver-white hair stepped out of the sun's glare. As I walked past him, he reached out and curled his fingers around my elbow, pulling me to a stop.

"When you get home, read Philippians 4:13," the man said matter-of-factly.

I blinked to bring the stranger into focus through moist eyes. "Excuse me?"

"When you get home, read Philippians 4:13," he repeated. The silver-haired man's gaze penetrated my soul. He smiled, dropped his hand from my arm and turned away.

Whirling around after him, I grabbed his arm. "Wait. Tell me what it says now. I have to know *now*," I demanded, desperate for any words of hope.

"I can do everything through Christ, who gives me strength."

"Thank you." Those were the only words that came to me. I breathed deeply and turned toward the exit again. I took only a step before turning back to thank the man one more time.

He wasn't there. Staring up and down the hallway, I searched for the silver-haired man who stood before me only a second ago. He had vanished. But where? There were no doors to duck into or corners to turn down. Only the elevator at the far end of the lobby. The bell rang to announce its arrival. When the door opened, passengers exited; no one waited to enter.

I shook my head and left the hospital. Inside my car, I rested my hands on the steering wheel and pondered my encounter with the silver-haired man who seemed to appear out of nowhere and vanish just as quickly.

His words of assurance echoed in my ears. A peace that had eluded me in a lonely hospital corridor outside my father-in-law's room now enveloped me.

✦ ✦ ✦ ✦ ✦

My father-in-law passed away two days later with our family at his side. Sadly, he slipped into a coma without ever allowing me to lead him in the believer's prayer. But I had glimpsed God's glory in a heavenly messenger.

I was comforted because God sent His special messenger to encourage and provide me the power to speak the doctor's words to my father-in-law's family. God assigned me a job for which I was ill-equipped. And that experience reminded me, the battle was His. I took my position, and He equipped me fully with his strength to do what He called me to do.

I was able to do that–just as the silver-haired messenger had promised.

CHAPTER THIRTY-ONE

Tokyo Angel

Elise Douglass Schneider

When my family and friends learned that my new position as provost of the Ventura County Community College District in California entailed my traveling throughout the world, often alone, they howled with laughter.

"What a sense of humor God has to send you," my husband said. "You often get lost reaching a new destination within twenty miles in Ventura County and you're going around the world to recruit international students?"

My friends joined in with comments such as, "And it's not just one trip but at least thirty spanning a six-year period—and some trips will extend fifty days."

I was about to leave on my first trip to Tokyo. I enthusiastically mapped out my schedule to visit seven international student agents throughout Japan. Those agents assisted students in selecting and applying for the three colleges I represented—Ventura, Moorpark, and Oxnard.

After I boarded the plane at Los Angeles I prayed for God's help, and especially that I wouldn't get lost. "Please help me not lose the agent's address."

From the airport I took a taxi to the hotel adjacent to the subway station. Following a good night's sleep and breakfast, I was ready to go. I had the address in my hand. I walked over to a hotel clerk I'd overheard speaking English with a guest.

"Good morning. Perhaps you can help," I said. I laid out my map with my destination circled in red. "Can you please tell me which subway to take?"

Giving the same professional attention he'd given the other guests, he gave me specific directions. He pointed to the subway across the street and down about four hundred yards. He told me everything I was to do and it seemed simple enough.

I can do this, I muttered to myself. Once I was on the appropriate train, I thanked God. *You know my history of easily getting lost. Guide me, dear God. Show me the way to the agent's office.*

Minutes later I got off the train and looked around. I had the address in my hand but there was one problem—every sign was in Japanese. Not one was printed in English. I had memorized exactly one word in Japanese, *arigato*, which means *thank you*. To make sure I said it properly, I wrote it down as *R RE GOT TOE*.

What do I do now? I was on the verge of panic. I had an address but had no way to find it. I couldn't even ask anyone for directions. *Dear Lord, please help me. Send me a guide. Someone. An angel from heaven.*

I stared at the red circle on the large map I held waist high as though expecting to see a Start-Here sign magically appear.

Distracted from my map by someone wearing black shoes, I looked up. A Japanese man with an extremely kind face stood next to me. He pointed to the red circle on my map and then to himself several times. Apparently, he'd observed me scanning my map and my obvious distress.

Can it be? I wondered. *Is this someone whom I can trust—someone sent by God to help me reach my destination?* I wasn't afraid, but I still hesitated. Even though I had prayed for someone, I was shocked by such a quick answer to my plea.

He continued the pointing motions, and it was obvious he was offering to help. I knew only one word of Japanese; apparently he didn't know any English.

Yet on that street in Tokyo, two strangers communicated.

He took a step forward and indicated I was to follow, which I did. We walked nonstop, although occasionally he'd turn and smile at me and I returned his smile.

Ten minutes passed. Then fifteen. We were still walking. My watch told me it had been twenty minutes, and we still hadn't arrived at our destination.

Twenty-five minutes turned into forty. How much longer?

The next time I looked at my watch it had been forty-five minutes since he had indicated I should follow. I wasn't afraid, but I was getting tired of walking that far in heels. I also wondered, of course, if he knew where I wanted to go. *What if he takes me to the wrong place?*

No, I reminded myself. I had prayed and almost immediately this kind-faced man came to me.

I tried to figure out how to ask him, "How much farther?" Maybe if I pointed to my watch and made gestures. Just then, he touched my arm. His smile turned into a full grin as he pointed to an address in Japanese and English above an office door. He nodded and pointed again.

I had arrived.

Overjoyed with excitement, I faced him and bowed three times repeating my memorized "R RE GOT TOE" each time I bent down.

Someone came down the street and I held up my camera and motioned for him to take our picture. He spoke in Japanese—which I didn't understand—but it didn't matter because he took the camera from my hand. The stranger in the black shoes stood next to me, our bodies gently touched.

In a way I can't put into words, as we stood there, I felt the two of us were no longer strangers and yet I had spoken only one word to him.

As he started to walk away I thought of the biblical account of the three men who appeared to Abraham. (You'll find the full story in Genesis, chapter 18.) Their purpose was to announce that in one year, the elderly couple, Abraham and Sarah, would have a son. Like the three strangers, the man in black shoes "just happened to appear."

Most people consider those three visitors divine messengers from heaven, who came to the patriarch with a powerful message. Mine wasn't a message like the one they delivered, but God certainly did send a messenger to me. He was my angel, whether a spirit or a human.

"Thank You, Lord, for sending Your angel to escort me to my destination," I whispered.

CHAPTER THIRTY-TWO

Watchmen

Karen Barnes Jordan

We considered our neighborhood safe, and our nine-year-old son Adam often rode his bike with his friends. But our six-year-old daughter Tara stayed close to our home.

During our years spent attending seminary, we lived in low-income housing in a North Texas neighborhood, without any trees or much grass in the yards. Everyone had an almost identical, small house, with similar-colored bricks and roofing—tract housing at its best—and that's all we could afford.

Late one summer afternoon, Adam failed to show up for our evening meal. When he didn't respond to his dad's calls to come home, I asked Tara, "Will you go find your brother? Tell him to come home for dinner."

As she walked toward the door, I added, "Stay out of the street. And come straight home."

Tara skipped out the front door, excited about her assignment and the opportunity to tell her brother what to do.

A few minutes later, Adam bolted through the door—without Tara. So I asked him, "Where is your sister?"

"I raced her home and beat her here," Adam said.

I looked out the kitchen window toward our unfenced backyard and the adjoining sidewalk, but I couldn't see Tara. Concerned, I walked outside and looked in the front yard and the street in front of our house. I couldn't see our daughter. Panicked by her absence, I told my husband Dan, "I'm going to find Tara."

I jogged to the end of the sidewalk. When I turned the corner, I saw Tara throw a stick down and turn around toward me. Relieved, I demanded, "Where have you been?"

Startled by my sudden appearance and intensity, Tara said, "Sorry, Mommy."

"I told you that dinner was ready. What took you so long?" As I continued to probe Tara about her whereabouts during the last few minutes, tears filled her bright, green eyes. She said nothing until I calmed down.

"I saw Adam on his bicycle at the end of the street. So I followed him." She took a big breath and said, "A scary man stopped his car and rolled his window down."

My heart began to race, as I realized the danger my daughter might have encountered just a few moments earlier.

"The man wanted me to come over to his car," she explained. "But you told me to never talk to strangers. So I picked up a stick and started to walk away."

"You did the right thing," I said.

"The stranger said something to me, but I didn't understand him." A wrinkle appeared on Tara's forehead.

Where is this story going? I thought. *What just happened here?*

"The man looked behind me, and he acted scared. Then, he just drove off—real fast." Tara waved her hand, like she shooed a fly away.

"Thank You, Lord Jesus," I whispered.

Then Tara's story took a remarkable twist, "When I looked behind me, I saw two big men standing there, right behind where the car had stopped. They were watching me."

Tara's eyes brightened, as she continued to describe her protectors, "They wore white clothes. One of them had a big, gold sword with little drawings on the handle." Tara traced a line on the palm of her hand, as she recalled the etchings on the sword. "His sword was really long—from his waist to the ground." As Tara described the sword, she bent over to her side and reached to the ground with one hand and up toward the sky with the other.

I listened silently as Tara finished telling her story. "One of those big men smiled and told me not to be scared anymore. He told me to throw my stick down and go home. When I turned around, I saw you, Mommy."

I saw Tara throw down her stick, but I didn't see any men. What on earth had just happened to my daughter?

When we reached our front door, Dan opened it with a perplexed look on his face.

I said calmly, "Tell your daddy what happened."

Tara retold her experience. We didn't say much then but sat down and ate. Afterward, when Dan and I were alone, I asked, "What do you think about Tara's story?"

"I think two angels saved our daughter's life."

"I've never talked about angels to Tara, have you?" At that time and as far as we knew, Tara hadn't been exposed to any teaching that would lead her to make up such a tale.

We didn't share Tara's experience with many of our family and friends because we feared their doubts or their abilities to grasp what we understood as God's protection for our daughter. When I have shared the story, I've received mixed responses. Some rolled their eyes and hummed the theme to the *Twilight Zone*. Others asked diagnostic and psychological questions. However, a few believers accepted it as a true story of an angelic appearance that resulted in changing our family's understanding of God and the supernatural.

Later, while I searched the Scriptures for answers to my questions about Tara's visitation, I noted a similar story in Genesis 19, when God sent two men to protect Lot and his family and lead them to safety.

Could Tara's "two big men" be the same two messengers? I don't know. But since that day—more than thirty years ago—when I'm afraid or anxious, God reminds me of the two big men that He sent to protect my daughter and send her back home to safety.

CHAPTER THIRTY-THREE

Who Called?

Sandee Martin Drake

M y husband's object of pride, a red GMC pickup truck, felt like an old clunker as I drove along Interstate 40 toward Flagstaff, Arizona. There had been no choice of power steering or power brakes back in 1972. Even though the speed limit of fifty-five mph seemed fast at the time, I drove cautiously since our son Jason, only sixteen months old, sat in his car seat next to me.

Along with an overworked heater, the bright sun beaming through the front windshield provided a little more warmth. The air felt crisp and cold on a beautiful cloudless November morning. The weather people predicted our first snowstorm for the weekend. I wanted to get to town, finish my weekly grocery shopping, get back, and prepare our noon meal.

My husband Frank, who worked for the US Forest Service in the Williams office as a civil engineer, walked home for a made-from-scratch lunch, and he also liked to spend a little time with our son before I put Jason down for his afternoon nap.

Just then, the steering wheel turned rapidly and I couldn't hold it steady. The truck started sliding from one side of the road to the other, faster than I could control it. My heart pounded hard, and I felt really scared. I had to continue to hold on. Even though I pumped the brakes, it had no effect. The truck was out of control.

We were going to have an accident.

I let go of the wheel and wrapped myself around my son and his car seat as my body bumped up and down in my seat, saddled with a seatbelt. The truck went off the highway and down an incline. The bumping pushed my body against the steering wheel, then the door, and toward my son. No matter how bruised I became, I refused to let go of my son.

I must have passed out.

My next moment of awareness was even more frightening. I opened one eye and tried to open the other but I couldn't. My hands went to my eyes and then my head, and I realized I was covered in bandages. I tried to speak but no words came. I couldn't see anything. I closed my eye to try to figure out where I was and what had happened. A severe pain in my chest kept me from sitting up, and my legs felt numb.

Tears started falling down my bruised cheeks. I felt I was screaming but my words came out as a whisper. "Jason, Jason, where are you? Are you here?"

Frank's large, warm hand wiped the tears from my face. "He's fine now; don't worry. You must rest. You've been in an accident and you're in a hospital."

By sheer willpower I was able to open both my eyes and focus on his concerned face. My voice sounded unsure and shaky as I whispered, "I don't feel so good, Frank. My head and chest really hurt. And I don't hear Jason; where is he?"

"He's in another room. Luckily for him, there is only a tiny scratch on his cheek. You were lucky, dear, and I thanked God for your safety when the phone call came to the office." He leaned over to give me a hug and kiss.

"Can you tell me what happened?" I didn't hear his answer because I drifted off to sleep, probably induced by the medication.

As I drifted back into consciousness, I couldn't remember the accident, going to the hospital, or anything. *What happened?* Each time I pondered the question, I must have gone back to sleep while someone gave me the answer.

For two days I drifted in and out of consciousness, feeling nothing but severe pain in my arms, chest, head, and neck. A nurse brought Jason in to see me on the third day and I thanked God that he hadn't been hurt. I continued to say thank-You prayers to God for saving us from what could have been a terrible tragedy.

When I finally woke up for good, I listened to a terrific tale of inexplicable help.

A county sheriff had also been driving to Flagstaff. A veteran of many years of driving back and forth on the highway, he had only two years left until retirement. Yet, probably out of habit, he continued to look on both sides of the road as he drove. A crackling noise and a weak voice he didn't recognize came over his radio while he tried to dial in a clearer sound.

He pulled over and scratched his balding head, trying to get some semblance of understanding from what he heard. Most of the words were garbled, but it was something about a woman and baby in crisis up ahead of him on the other side of the road.

"Look up ahead. Hurry." He heard those words clearly.

The sheriff tried to get in touch with the main switchboard to learn what happened, but he could hear nothing except the repeated words, "Look up ahead; hurry." He pulled back onto the road and continued to drive east.

"Imagine my surprise when I looked ahead and saw, to my shock, a red pickup just off the road, front end down, back wheels spinning, and smoke coming out of the engine." He called for an ambulance as he drove over to the left side of the road and pulled off onto the rough ground. After he opened his door he heard a baby cry.

The sheriff went to the truck and carefully pulled both of us out. He realized I was hurt with the cuts and abrasions on my face and head. Jason had no visible sign of serious injuries, just one scratch on his cheek.

Later in the hospital, the officer told Frank, "I've tried repeatedly to find out about the mysterious call that came over my radio. No one from the station claims to have sent that message. Your wife must have been saved by her guardian angel."

I believe the county sheriff was right.

CHAPTER THIRTY-FOUR

Would an Angel Wear a Baseball Hat?

Geni J. White

I felt like a foolish failure. I'd burned the roast for our dinner when I didn't realize I'd set the oven temperature too high. Because of nasal-impacting allergies, I have a limited sense of smell. Smoke sneaking from the oven door finally alerted me to our dinner's disaster.

After that, I accidentally deleted a dozen important computer files. Although I joke about gremlins in my computer, the real fault was my shaky fingers that hit the wrong keys.

That wasn't all. The bathroom floor flooded when the toilet backed up. Had a visiting neighbor child stuffed too much toilet tissue down the bowl? I assumed it was something like that. Mopping robbed me of valuable time for dinner preparations. My husband Bob had an important meeting that evening and couldn't be late.

I cleaned the bathroom floor by pushing around old towels under my feet, mopping the tiles with soapy water, and mopping it again with bleach.

My mood grew darker from insidious inner whispers. "You're a miserable human specimen. You can't even cook a good dinner and serve it on time. Even God couldn't love you." The accuser worked overtime on me that day, but I didn't waken to the onslaught's source until that afternoon when I met the extraordinary tall fellow in the baseball cap.

I'd felt especially blue thinking my husband might leave home hungry if I didn't cook dinner on time–and my cupboard was empty of decent, quick-meal fixings. Finally overcoming sighs of irritation, I drove to Costco. Traffic and a heavy rain slowed my trip.

After buying my groceries, including salad ingredients and a rotisserie chicken, I unloaded the full cart into the car trunk with one hand, while trying vainly in the downpour to position my umbrella over cardboard containers of cereals and pastas.

Finally I was ready to inch my way along the busy streets to home. Uh-oh. I'd forgotten to pick up salad dressing. And I was out of money. Fortunately, I had a coupon for a free bottle from a different store.

Traffic crawled along as I drove nearly a mile to Safeway. Just as I pulled up to park, I discovered I didn't have my billfold. It wasn't in any pockets of my jacket or jeans. It wasn't under the car seat or on the car floor. I carefully removed and replaced groceries to be sure but it wasn't in the trunk either.

I tried to focus on everything I had done with my billfold. That's when I remembered setting the gold-colored leather billfold in the basket of my shopping cart while I unloaded groceries at Costco. That way I'd have a hand free for the umbrella to shield me from the rain. I groaned.

Now at nearly a snail's speed because of traffic, I had to drive that crowded street back to Costco. More time lost. My prayer during that agonizing trip in pouring rain was desperate. "Please, Lord, let me find my billfold."

My shopping cart still sat where I'd abandoned it, tilted from two wheels on the sidewalk. Had the weather kept employees from gathering carts quickly?

To my shock, my billfold rested in the basket, soaking up rain, but everything inside was still dry. With a grateful heart, I thanked the Lord.

The trip back to Safeway was nail-chewingly slow. Inside the store, I rushed along the salad aisle, eyeing every shelf and every brand, but couldn't find the particular brand of dressing my coupon offered.

Then the extratall man appeared at my side. "Are you looking for Ken's Salad Dressing?"

"Why, yes." *How did he know?*

I didn't notice much about him except that he was so tall his shoulders towered above me, and his chin was much higher than the top shelf at the grocery store. His arms stretched easily to the back of that shelf. He wore a white baseball hat turned backward. I have no idea what team. I was so frazzled I only vaguely observed a red-and-gold logo.

"It's here." The man's voice was calm and pleasant. His long arms reached clear to the back of the top shelf. "Only two bottles left. Creamy Caesar Salad Dressing, I believe you want?"

"Oh yes." I was mentally blown away by his question. And I'd never have spotted or reached the bottle on that high shelf.

The man handed me the dressing. I glanced at the jar, then up at the fellow to thank him. He wasn't in sight anywhere along the salad aisle. *How could anyone dash down that long aisle so fast? Was this guy some Olympic runner in town incognito?*

I scurried to the end of the row and scanned both adjacent aisles. No man was there, only a few women. *How strange.* I headed toward checkout thinking surely I'd spot that tall, baseball-hat-covered head above all the grocery shelves.

But I didn't see him.

At first I was confused, but then a strange idea drifted into my dithering brain. Would God have sent an angel to help me, especially for such a little thing as locating one bottle of salad dressing?

The Bible says the Lord also counts the hairs on my head (Matthew 10:30). Hairs are especially small things, but God is aware.

Could that have been—was that man really an angelic being sent just to me from the Lord? As I drove home through the rain, my spirits lifted. That tall man–just doing the simple thing of anticipat-ing what I wanted and pointing it out to me–changed my thinking. If God cared enough to send someone to point out the location of salad dressing, surely the Lord cared about everything in my life.

Maybe I wasn't such a miserable human specimen. Maybe God truly loved me.

Back home, I served my husband a great Caesar salad and roasted chicken thighs before he left for his meeting. And I thanked God that He'd sent along someone to show He still cared for me, no matter how unworthy I felt or how terribly the day had gone.

I've never forgotten that unusual tall man. Ever since meeting him I've believed that God truly cares about small things–like a need for salad dressing. Remembering that little things are important to God has encouraged me for years. I'm also more aware of accusing inner voices, to shut them up faster. That surely was an important part of God's lessons for me that day.

CHAPTER THIRTY-FIVE

Lost in New York City

Mary Cantell

On a cool, May morning in my senior year of high school, I stood with a group of about twenty classmates aboard a packed elevated train in New York City. My first trip to the Big Apple. Our creative writing teacher, Mrs. Hutson, thought it would be helpful for the class–especially the want-to-be journalists–to visit Columbia University where we would attend the Columbia Scholastic Press Association for two days of workshops and seminars.

"This is our stop," she called out as the train squealed and slowed. "Everybody stick together."

The doors slid open and everyone, including the New York commuters, rushed toward the narrow exit like sand through an hourglass. I brought up the rear, and before I could exit, the glass doors slammed shut inches from my face.

"Mary!" I heard my friend Kevin call from the platform, looking aghast at my predicament.

Others turned to stare, including Mrs. Hutson. I shrugged and smiled to let them know I wasn't upset at the situation, then raised my hand in a tiny wave in the seconds before the train lurched away.

Deeper and deeper into New York City I went, sitting alone by the window. I felt I was having an adventure. Red building. White warehouse. The staccato of colors flashed as the train swept through town. I should have been worried, I suppose, but I wasn't and was sure the train would eventually have to double back. I'd get off then and try to find Columbia University. There was no need to panic. The train stopped once, twice, and after the third stop, something urged me to get off.

I stepped off the subway. The street looked like any other city street, lined with storefronts. After walking a few blocks, I wondered just how far I was from Columbia University. Stepping inside one of the stores, I walked to the back where a woman stood behind a worn wooden counter assisting a customer. The floor was covered with sawdust.

"Excuse me, but can you tell me where I am?"

The woman stopped what she was doing and stared at me. She crinkled her eyes as though perplexed–not at the question so much as at me. In a decisive tone like I should know better, she told me.

Thanking her, I left the store and continued walking up Lenox Avenue. I was in Harlem.

Several blocks ahead, a group of tough-looking guys hung around the front steps of a brick row house. A couple of them stared at me as I approached. Something glinted in one man's hand. Was it a knife? A key? A stick of gum in a thin foil wrapper? I didn't want it to be a knife, but it probably was.

Feigning a courage I didn't own, I kept my stride and prayed silently, hoping my fears weren't holding up a neon sign somewhere above my head. Every inch of my body braced to flee.

No one bothered me.

It seemed like miles had passed along Lenox Avenue before the greenery of Central Park beckoned in the near distance. As I began to find my bearings, at least my bearings as to where the hotel was, a sense of peace returned. I had no idea where to find Columbia University.

I'd had enough for one morning and decided to go back to the hotel. I waited on the curb for several cars to pass. When all was clear, and just before stepping into the street, someone grabbed my arm. I turned to see a tall man in an overcoat; his face was partly shaded by his collar. He pulled me back from entering the street just as a bus zoomed past, leaving a wake of exhaust fumes.

"Thank you," I said, somewhat embarrassed at not noticing the bus. "I didn't even see—"

He was gone.

I didn't understand it. I had seen the man. He had grabbed me.

✦ ✦ ✦ ✦ ✦

Later that afternoon, I caught up with my classmates. We gathered in Mrs. Hutson's room where Kevin and others peppered me with questions. *What happened? Where'd you go?*

As I recounted the course of my eventful morning, Mrs. Hutson looked at me with a doubtful expression.

"Lenox Avenue?" she said, shaking her head. "You did *not* walk down Lenox Avenue."

"Yes, I did."

"No way," she said as she reached for a cigarette. "Oh, Mary, there's no way you did that." She took a drag and blew the smoke out, still shaking her head.

I stood stunned at her insistence that I was lying. What was there to lie about?

"I walked down Lenox Avenue. What's the big deal?" I said, accenting the last two words.

Later, I came to know the big deal. *It was dangerous.* Even in daylight. Mrs. Hutson was a New Yorker, and she knew.

While I understood her skepticism, I also believed her mindset would probably preclude her from understanding what *really* happened that morning and what kept me safe on those city streets. If she didn't believe something as tangible as my walk down Lenox

Avenue, what would be her take on the possibility of an intangible spirit–perhaps a guardian angel who had saved me from being hit by a bus?

Since childhood, I'd heard about guardian angels, but until that "man" pulled me back, I had never experienced one personally. At least, not consciously.

In hindsight, maybe I should have shared my thoughts with her. *God sent an angel, Mrs. Hutson, to protect me every step of the way.*

There'll always be skeptics like Mrs. Hutson, and I probably can't change their thinking. But I changed my thinking. An unseen angel had walked with me and a seen angel had grabbed me so a bus wouldn't hit me.

I believe in angels.

CHAPTER THIRTY-SIX

Angel in the Airport

Jean Matthew Hall

A hurricane? You've got to be kidding me," Francie said after she heard the weather report. "Our little motel room has that huge window. We can't stay there. We have to get out of this place."

I wasn't as worried, but I wanted both of us to be at peace. It was August 1995, and my assistant Francie and I were in Pensacola, Florida, for professional training–the week Hurricane Erin made landfall at the same place.

After checking out of our motel, Francie and I stopped at a convenience store and bought snacks, bottles of water, and flashlights, before we joined several hundred "campers" in the lobbies of the Student Center on the conference grounds.

And it was a wise decision. We spent the remainder of that day and night at the hurricane-proof windows watching Erin uproot ancient oak trees and rip the roofs off nearby houses. By midnight the hurricane had headed inland. Even though Erin left massive property damage behind, as we learned later, there had been no casualties.

Francie and I spent another exhausting night on the floor of the Student Center. Then we bought more snacks and water, and headed for the small Pensacola airport.

"I'm exhausted," I said after we turned in the rental car. "And I sure don't want to ride out another hurricane tonight at this airport."

"Yeah, but there's not much we can do about it," Francie said.

"Except pray," I said. So we held hands and prayed.

The lines outside the Pensacola airport were unbelievable. We stepped to the end of a line that snaked its way from the parking lot and through the terminal doors.

When we finally made it inside the terminal, we realized that all flights had been cancelled for two days. Hundreds of stranded travelers were crammed together. Every rental car in the city headed north. The computer system and electrical power at the airport had been out of commission and had only begun to function shortly before we arrived. Phone lines and power lines were down all over the city.

The airlines tried to reschedule flights, squeeze extra people onto every vacant seat of the already scheduled flights, and manage a messed-up maze of arrivals and departures. The airport staff cleaned debris off runways, while others searched for lost luggage.

On the televised news we learned that a second tropical storm was tracking right behind Erin. It was scheduled to make landfall in Pensacola that very night, so travelers scrambled to get out of town as fast as they possibly could.

In the middle of the confusion a man wearing a crisp black-and-white uniform stepped up to the counter. He had a calmness about him and appeared oblivious to the craziness all through the terminal. He punched a few keys on a computer and his gaze scanned the crowd.

He looked straight at Francie and me, nodded to us, and beckoned us to come to him. We looked around. Not another person in line had noticed. It was as if he were invisible to everyone but us. He motioned again.

Francie and I grabbed our luggage and zigzagged our way toward him. No one spoke to us or tried to stop us. I wondered, *Am I dreaming this?*

We stepped up to the counter and handed the man our tickets. He smiled and explained that they would do their best to get us out of Pensacola before nightfall. He seemed calm and refreshed while his counterparts all over the airport looked exhausted.

I wanted to call him by name, and realized that his ID badge, clipped below his pocket, had been turned around so I could see only the back side. He was the only airport employee whose name I couldn't read.

He handed us our boarding passes and asked that we hold onto our luggage. Then he stepped aside and opened a small employees-only gate. He motioned us through. As we walked to the boarding area, Francie looked at me with a huge question mark in her eyes. She whispered, "What's he doing?"

"I don't know," I said, "but don't lose sight of him."

The man showed us where to wait. Then he tipped the polished bill of his cap and disappeared into the crowd.

The waiting area was packed with weary vacationers, crying babies, and frustrated mommies. It was noisy and hot because the air-conditioning had been knocked out by the storm. We found a spot near an agent and sat on our suitcases to wait. Francie leaned against the wall and closed her eyes. I tried to read, but I soon used my book as a fan instead.

Several times the PA system crackled, and an anonymous voice asked passengers to surrender their seats in exchange for free passes on Saturday or Sunday. The airlines tried to get people from earlier cancelled flights out of the city first. However, with the threat of another storm headed for Pensacola only a handful of travelers took them up on the offer.

In the middle of a "Flight so-and-so is now boarding at Gate 2" announcement, the man in the crisp black-and-white uniform came toward us again. He stopped and whispered to the agent standing near Francie and me. Again, I noticed that his ID badge was turned backward.

I nudged Francie. "Look, that man is back."

He turned and nodded at me, smiled, and melted into the crowd. The attendant picked up her microphone.

"Passenger Jean Hall and her party please report to Gate 12. Your flight is now boarding. Jean Hall, report immediately to Gate 12."

"Francie, that's us. Come on, we have a flight out." We stood up, grabbed our bags, and ran toward the gate.

We raced up to Gate 12 and waved our passes at the haggard attendant. Between breaths we laughed and asked each other what in the world had just happened. We hurried down the boarding corridor. At the door of the airplane we shoved our passes into the waiting hand of a weary flight attendant and then plowed down the aisle searching for our seats. After we stashed our bags overhead we plopped down, exhausted, but exuberant.

"Isn't this amazing? It's like that man was sent just to help us. It couldn't be a coincidence that he showed up *twice*. And look—we're on a flight," Francie said.

"Looks like God answered our prayers," I said with a yawn. "We're headed for Atlanta and then home."

"Hey, did you notice that you couldn't see his ID badge?" she asked.

"Yes," I said. "Twice I looked. I almost asked but I didn't want to interrupt him."

"It was almost as if he didn't *have* a name," she said.

"It's sure unusual that an airline employee wouldn't show his ID badge," I said.

"You don't suppose . . ."

"Suppose what?" I asked.

Francie lowered her voice. "You don't suppose he was an *angel*, do you?"

The engines whined, and we backed away from the terminal.

"I don't think angels always appear to us with halos and feathered wings," I said. "I believe God sends them to us in a form that meets our needs."

Francie smiled. "You mean like regular people? Like maybe airline people?"

"Like regular people," I said and smiled.

"I've never met a real angel before," she said. "I never even had God answer a prayer like that for me before."

"God cares about us."

"I know that now. But I didn't realize God is even concerned about my everyday needs. I thought He rescued us from big things like cancer and danger."

"Nothing is too small for God to be concerned about. . . . Whatever concerns us, concerns Him."

As we continued our flight, I kept thinking about that experience. *Why us? The terminal was filled with people, and none of them could get out. Why us? What made us deserve special treatment?*

I don't have an answer, but I have learned one important thing. We didn't deserve special consideration, but God smiled on us.

We call that grace, don't we?

CHAPTER THIRTY-SEVEN

Angel Glacier

Janice Rice

Few things in my childhood were more fun than getting together with my cousins from Canada. One summer break, when I was about eight years old, we traveled to the "Great White North" to visit my relatives. We decided to take a day hike to Jasper National Park in Alberta to see the glaciers.

Our older cousins and my brother Chris and I took off ahead of our parents along a snow-packed trail up into the mountains. We ran a good mile or two up the path. An iced-over lake was to the right of the path. We stopped for a breather and scanned the frozen surface next to us.

"I want to go ice skating," one cousin said.

"Me too," said another.

"But the ice might crack," my brother said. "How do you know it can hold you?"

"We'll just have to test it, that's all," someone else reasoned. "Who's the smallest one here?" I volunteered. I was the smallest one, so who else should test the ice, but me? Not only was I a bit of a show-off, I was also the youngest in the group and felt the constant need to be accepted.

As my cousins and big brother cheered me on, I slid one tentative foot onto the ice. It was holding. I slid my foot out a bit farther and stepped off the snowy pathway onto the ice.

I inched out still farther, waved, and yelled, "Come on, you guys, it's—"

Then I screamed as I broke through the cracking ice into freezing water. A thousand needles seemed to pierce my skin through my clothing as I sank into the glacial runoff. I was already in water too deep for me to touch bottom. My drenched clothes clung to me, weighing me down. I hung onto the edge of the broken ice.

"Help!" I pleaded with my cousins and brother on shore. "Help me out!"

"We can't, Janice! We'll fall through," one cousin yelled back to me.

Even as scared as I was, I could see the terror in their eyes.

I spun around in the water, clawing at the rough icy surface, trying to grab hold of anything to pull myself out. The ice kept breaking around me into a wider circle. The more I tried to climb out, the bigger the hole of broken ice became.

"Help! Somebody, help!" I screamed, bitterly cold and desperate. "I can't hold on much longer!"

No adults were around. My cousins and brother wouldn't leave me but they couldn't help me either.

Just then, a man wearing running shorts and a tank top came around the corner. *He must really be cold with no long pants on*, I thought.

The man ran to where my cousins and brother stood. He didn't stop, but he slowed down and walked out onto the ice. He leaned over and grabbed me under the arms.

I stared, unable to believe he was standing on the ice. He dragged me out of the broken hole and back to the pathway. He stood me on my feet. "Are you all right?" he asked.

Despite being soaked and totally chilled, I nodded.

He backed up a few steps.

I was soaked and began shivering and shaking uncontrollably. My brother and cousins sprang into action, huddled around me and offered me their clothes.

The runner sternly looked from one child to another. "Don't go out there again."

All of us shook our heads.

"I won't ever do that again," I said." I promise."

The others also assured the man that they wouldn't go out on the ice.

The runner smiled, turned, and took off running up the snowy path. He left me standing with the others, dripping wet, in shock, but alive.

We all stared after the runner in disbelief. Then reality hit us.

"He walked on the ice," my brother said.

"He . . . he didn't break through the ice," my cousin said.

"How did he walk out there?" another cousin asked. "Janice broke through and she's the smallest."

They tried to figure it out but I stopped them with my frantic plea. "I'm freezing to death!" My wet clothes clung to me and were so heavy I had trouble walking. The rough, frozen denim scratched my legs like a million bee stings as I shuffled back to the path and toward my parents. Painful knots in my muscles took over as I put one foot in front of the other.

They temporarily forgot about the runner and helped me get back to our family.

I reached my parents with crunchy, frozen hair. My clothes had rubbed my skin raw while I walked. Dad grabbed my icy hand in his and led me back to the car to find dry clothes. I didn't have to stick around for the scolding the mothers gave my brother and cousins.

"Dad," I said, through chattering teeth, "know what?"

"What, Janice?" he said hurriedly, trying to get me to warmth and safety.

"A man saved me," I said.

"Really?"

My dad kept moving me along at a good clip. I wanted him to carry me because I was so tired and cold, but he forced me to walk to keep me warm.

"Yes," I continued. "A man in running shorts *sa-sa-sa-saved* me." My teeth chattered.

"A man in running shorts? Are you sure?"

"He walked right out on the ice and pu-pu-pulled me out."

"But you broke through," my dad said, staring at me.

"Yes, kinda crazy, huh?"

I don't remember much else about that day except that the kids weren't allowed to run ahead anymore. We eventually saw the source of the glacier we were looking for, but I was to stay only for a few minutes after my long hike.

The name of the glacier we visited in Jasper National Park is called the Angel Glacier.

I'll never forget that adventure.

CHAPTER THIRTY-EIGHT

Our Umbrella Angel

Donna Sherer

Most of my evenings started out like those of many families with small children, fighting the unending battle of "the stall." My four-year-old son Brendan was the master of stall tactics, never ceasing to amaze me at his creativity. His sister Elizabeth, who was just under a year old, unknowingly helped out by being a fussy baby at night. My son would insist that his sister was crying because she wanted him to stay up and watch a movie with her, sing to her, or rock her.

That particular evening had started to resemble the others, but my son came up with something brilliant. He turned on the Weather Channel. Even though the weather was clear outside at the time, he heard the word *storm.* "Are we going to have a storm tonight? Look at all those colors on the map. Are those colors bad?"

He looked up at me with nothing short of fear in his little eyes and said with a tremble in his voice, "I'm scared."

His tactic worked, and my heart melted. As I balanced my crying baby on one leg, I pulled Brendan into my lap and cuddled him close. "Is Sissy crying because she's scared too?" he asked.

I took a deep breath before I began my response. "She's crying because her tummy hurts." I stared at the TV screen again. "You know, that storm does look pretty big on that map."

"It sure does."

"Do you remember the Bible story we read the other day about Jesus and his friends being in a boat? Jesus fell asleep and a big storm came up. The wind was really bad and the waves were big. His friends were scared."

He smiled. "Sure I do, Mommy. Jesus told the storm to stop and it did. But, Mommy, Jesus is not sleeping in our house."

"That's true, but Jesus knows when there is going to be a storm and He'll look out for us. Don't be afraid, Jesus will take care of us."

About that time, the back door opened and my husband Kevin came inside. Our son jumped up and ran to meet him. His attention had been diverted, so I went back to comforting our daughter. Kevin has a great way with our children, and it wasn't long before our son was off to bed without another word about the coming storm.

A few hours passed and just as predicted by the Weather Channel, the storm moved into our area. I had finally gotten my daughter to sleep and I was hoping that both children would sleep right through whatever noise the weather made.

Kevin and I talked about our day until he was ready for bed. He kissed me good night and headed off into the back of the house. I had to finish washing the baby bottles. "I'll be there shortly," I said.

The wind had begun to increase as lightning flashed and thunder rumbled. So far, no one was awakened by the commotion. I turned off the light and started down the hallway. I looked in on the children, tucked in their beds, sleeping soundly. As I finally lay down myself, I released a deep sigh.

Just then, a flash of lightning, bright enough to light up the whole house, was followed immediately by heavy thunder that shook the windows.

Both children screamed, and we jumped out of bed. Kevin went to get our daughter and I went to our son.

"That was so loud," Brendan said. "I'm really scared. Are we going to be okay?"

"Sure we will," I said. "And don't forget, Jesus is watching out for us."

He wrapped his arms around my neck as tightly as he could as we walked up the hall and sat down on the couch next to my husband and daughter.

It was precious to watch our little boy try to comfort his sister's crying, while he was fighting back his own tears. "We will be okay. Jesus is watching out for us."

All four of us sat in the dark–two terrified kids and two extremely tired parents. My husband and I both enjoy watching thunderstorms, so we didn't turn on the lights. I think we were both praying that our son would see that we were composed and that would calm him down. But as the storm got worse, even we began to get a little tense.

To take the children's attention away from the severity of the storm, we started watching the shadows on the floor made by the tree limbs just outside the window. Their limbs twisted and danced in most unnatural ways. This seemed to work, until there was a crash of thunder that once again frightened both of the children.

Just then, my son sat straight up on the couch. He tilted his head to the right, then the left. "Look. Do you see him?" Jumping off the couch, he ran over to the window and pointed to the tree in the front yard.

My husband and I looked at each other before we stared out the window. We didn't see anything unusual.

Our son turned around and smiled. "It's going to be fine. Jesus is watching out for us, all right. He put an angel in the tree to guard our house." He turned and headed back to his bedroom.

My husband and I had been praying for about an hour and the unexpected words stunned us. "An angel is in the tree?" my husband asked.

"Sure is, Daddy. Don't you see him?"

"Tell Mommy and me where to look. What does he look like? We don't want to miss seeing him."

"You can't miss him. He's really big. He's right there," he said as he pointed out the window again. "He's sitting on that limb and he has huge wings. He has them over our house like an *ungrella*."

"An umbrella? The angel has his wings over our house like an umbrella?"

"Yes, Daddy, an *ungrella*. Mommy, you were right. Jesus put an angel out there to look out for us. I'm not scared anymore. I think I'll go to bed now. I love you, Mommy." He kissed me on the cheek and said, "Daddy, come tuck me in." He pulled his father down to the bedroom.

I sat there for a long time trying to picture the angel with the umbrella wings sitting in our tree as I rocked my daughter back to sleep. As the storm passed through, everyone in the house slept peacefully, knowing we were under the angel's umbrella.

A couple of years passed and we moved from that house into an apartment in another city. Our family had only mentioned the umbrella angel once or twice during those years, but the lasting effect on our son was evident.

One night we had a severe storm. This storm was in the spring and had the potential of becoming a tornado. That's when I got nervous. As we sat in the living room, the kids played and my husband read while I kept an eye out the sliding glass door.

I left the room for a few minutes. When I returned, Brendan, now six, and Elizabeth, almost three, stood and stared out the glass door. Our son turned and said matter-of-factly, "Look, Mom, the angel is back."

"Sure is," Elizabeth said.

I tried not to look too amazed, but apparently I didn't do a good job. My little girl smiled at me and said, "He's over by the trees. Don't you see him?"

My husband and I just looked at each other and smiled. How kind of God to allow my children to see His protection for us, and be able to let my husband and me know that we are covered by a truly weatherproof umbrella.

CHAPTER THIRTY-NINE

Bats in Our Belfry

Terri Elders

A few years ago I returned to Scotts Mills, Oregon. I'd spoken at a school counselors' conference a few hours' drive from there, so I seized the opportunity to revisit the town where I'd met my first miracle.

I'd heard that the Willamette Valley hadn't changed much, but that many of the old houses in the little hamlets surrounding Silverton had burned to the ground. I wouldn't have been surprised to see a modern bungalow or even a duplex on the grounds where I used to live.

When I got to the crest of the hill at Sixth and Grandview, I gasped in delight. The old Victorian house still stood, one of the few remaining homes from the town's 1890s heyday. More than sixty years earlier I'd lived in that house with my grandparents, parents, sister, and brother.

I walked around the front of the property, thanking God I'd had the chance to see the place again. The maple and cherry trees had grown higher, of course, and the barn wore a new coat of paint. Otherwise I could have shut my eyes and been transported back to the 1940s.

When my family moved there from Southern California after World War II, I'd chosen the unfinished storage room at the end of the second-story hallway as my playroom. I propped my dolls atop the cardboard boxes lining the walls, and pretended to teach them to read. When I tired of their lack of cooperation, I curled up on the cot in the corner and read.

One warm, late afternoon I fell asleep over the classic children's book *Hans Brinker or the Silver Skates*. I'd dreamed I was Gretel, skating gracefully down the canal alongside my brother, pacing my glides to the muffled squeals in the background, little kissy sounds like Mama made when she called the cat. Then something soft and silky caressed my cheek. I opened my eyes to see a cloud of bats circle overhead before they fluttered out the open window.

I shrieked loudly and seconds later footsteps pounded down the hall. Grandma and Mama burst into the room.

Grandma grabbed my arm. "What on earth is going on? You sounded like a banshee."

"Banshee? What's a banshee? No, there were bats," I said, waving toward the window. "Bats, a bunch of them, and they woke me up."

Grandma sat down on the cot next to me. "Are you certain?"

"There were four or five, and one of them touched me."

"They didn't hurt you." Grandma winked at Mama as her way of saying they should just humor me. "There's macaroni and cheese, and I made an apple pie for dessert."

I quieted down. I didn't like it that Grandma and Mama apparently didn't believe me. The macaroni was something I did like and so I temporarily forgot the bats.

That evening I asked Mama if I could tell people that we had bats in our belfry.

"No," Mama said and chuckled. "We don't have a belfry, just an attic. A belfry is a bell tower, like the one at the Friends Church."

Close enough, I thought, making a mental note to talk with my Sunday school teacher. The following Sunday I asked Miss Magee if the church had bats in its belfry. One thing I really liked about her is that she always took my questions seriously. Yet I could see her struggling to hide a smile. I wondered what was funny. Surely bats were more scary than amusing.

"I've seen them around the bell tower at night," she said. "They live in most of the old houses around here too. But don't be scared of bats. They're helpful. They eat insects, clean their fur like cats, and protect farmers' fields against rootworm. We should be grateful for them, just as we are for many of God's creatures."

"And what's a banshee?" I'd been puzzled ever since Grandma said I sounded like one.

"Oh, child, don't worry about banshees. My family came from Ireland, and they used to claim that banshees come from the otherworld and wail if someone is about to die. But they're like fairies and elves, all make-believe. Guardian angels are real."

I was glad I'd asked, because Miss Magee knew just about everything. I'd be able to sleep more easily now and not have to worry about anything evil disturbing my dreams. I looked forward to seeing more of the bats, and sometimes even pretended to fall asleep on the corner cot. The bats avoided the storage room the rest of the summer.

One nippy autumn night, tucked safely in my bed, I once again dreamed of hearing that strange chatter and chirp that sounded like baby kisses. A sweet voice called out, "Wake up. Wake up."

I opened my eyes but had to squint against the sting of smoke. Coughing, I scrambled to the window to let air into the room. The house was on fire!

Through the thick gray haze I glimpsed two or three tiny, silvery-winged shapes wafting through the window into the night. Must be bats, I thought, as I stumbled into the hallway.

"Grandma! Grandpa! Mama! Daddy! Get up! The house is on fire," I screamed. Everybody rushed from their bedrooms into the hall and rushed down the stairs, gagging and hacking.

"The particleboard caught fire," Daddy yelled to us. He and Grandpa grabbed bathroom towels, soaked them in the sink, and slapped them against the walls on either side of the fireplace. Grandma and Mama ran from room to room, throwing open the downstairs windows to let the smoke escape.

They stopped the fire before it did any serious damage.

"It must have been the bats that woke me up," I said, once we were certain that our house wouldn't be the latest Victorian to go up in flames. A house nearby had burned down just a few weeks earlier, the second that year.

"Bats?" Mama asked. "What do you mean?

"I heard them in my dream. They called my name. They told me to wake up."

"They must have been looking for an escape from the house," Grandpa said, giving me a strange look. "But how did they get into your bedroom? Your door was closed."

"I don't know, but they did."

That was the end of the discussion at home. I wasn't sure anyone believed me, but it was all right: *I knew the truth.*

The next Sunday when I told Miss Magee that bats had saved our house from burning down, she frowned. "Bats? You saw bats?"

"My room was very smoky. But they had wings. And they called my name."

She grinned. "Talking bats?"

"What else could they be?" I asked. "I'm too old to believe in fairies."

"Just think: which of God's creatures have wings, can talk, and don't need an open door or window to get into a room?" Miss

Magee clasped my hand. "Don't you remember what I told you about guardian angels? There's somebody watching out for you."

A guardian angel. My own guardian angel.

I stared at her and thought I could count on Miss Magee to have the answers.

"You've got to have faith that there's more to the world than what can be explained," she said. "Miracles happen. God's love is miraculous and shows itself in what seems to us to be magical."

Miracles, angels, and magic. That made sense to me then. And it does even today.

CHAPTER FORTY

Angels Unaware

Mary Salisbury Skeens

I had finished my grocery shopping and was eager to get home and out of the relentless heat. The Florida summer sun was ten degrees hotter than normal for that time of year and it wrapped the parking lot in a stifling blanket of humidity. Sweat dripped off the end of my nose as I tried repeatedly to insert my key into the ignition. Something was blocking it. Had I damaged the key? A faulty ignition? I had no idea.

Finally, giving up, I decided to call for a tow truck before the pounding heat ruined my groceries or I fainted.

I grabbed my purse, and fumbled past my checkbook, house keys, and grocery lists looking for my cell phone. It wasn't there.

I must have left it at home. I wasn't sure what to do. Pay phones aren't around the way they used to be.

I got out of the car and started into the store. Right in front of the entrance were two telephones. I picked up one but there was no dial tone. None on the second either. I turned around just as an employee pushed a line of grocery carts to the entrance. "Excuse me, why don't these phones work?"

"They've been moved from somewhere inside the store." He stared at me as if I had lost my mind. "Someone put them there for people from the phone company to collect them."

"Is there a live phone somewhere? I can't find my cell phone and–"

"Customer Service might be able to help you." He shrugged and continued pushing the carts.

I glared at him as he went by as if it wasn't his problem. Realizing my terrible attitude I said, "Lord, I'm sorry. Help me not to have a temper tantrum. But, please, help me. I don't know what to do."

I was about to lose a week's groceries to the heat of a punishing sun. Where is God in this? What happened to Jesus' promise to be with us always?

I stood in front of the store, trying to decide whether to go inside and ask for help. It was the end of the week and the store was packed with people. Yet going inside was the only sensible thing to do.

I entered the store, headed for the end of what seemed like an endless line that curved out from the counter marked Customer Service.

"Go to K-Mart."

I thought I was hearing things and kept on walking.

"Go to K-Mart."

I have no idea where that voice came from but I knew I had to obey. I turned around, left the crowded store, and walked quickly toward K-Mart at the other end of the strip mall.

Despite the feeling of being in a sun-bathed sauna, I walked as if someone had fastened a leash around my collar. I reached the department store, wiped moisture off my face, and stood bewildered while the clerk finished with her customer.

"Can I help you?" The blonde woman looked at me with friendly eyes just as if she'd been expecting me.

"Sorry to bother you." I took a deep breath and the words tumbled out. "I left home without my cell phone and the car won't start. I desperately need to call a tow truck and I tried to–"

She slid a console model toward me. "Will this do?"

"Yes, oh yes." I pulled a tissue from my purse and wiped my shaky hands off and stared at the mind-boggling buttons in front of me. "I haven't used one of these in a long time."

"I'll get an outside line for you," she said as if I were the only person on earth. She dialed a number and handed me the phone. "I need to call information to find the number for a towing service."

After I found the number, she smiled and listened while I explained that the ignition had mysteriously locked up and I couldn't get the key to turn. "Now I'm stranded in a parking lot with a load of groceries that are melting in the hot sun." I gave her the location of the car.

"As soon as we can locate a tow truck, we'll send it," the voice said. "It's a hot day and many drivers are experiencing problems."

My heart sank. My fixed income allowed few extra expenditures each month and my perishable goods were gathering E. coli in the sun. Chicken and hamburger were thawing. I hated to think of any of the other perishables inside the steaming car.

Depressed, I hung up and handed her the telephone. "Thank you."

As I started toward the door, I had an idea. I'd spend my last few dollars on bags of ice and a cooler. Maybe that would avoid the spoilage.

"Wait! Don't go away," the woman called. "I know someone who can help you." She made a call and less than a minute later, a tall, elderly man walked up to me.

"Let me help you." He listened to my story and said, "Let me take a look."

We hurried to my car through unwavering heat and hot winds. The man opened the door, bent down, and did some kind of manipulating to the brake and the gear shift. "That releases the locked-up steering wheel," he said. He inserted the key into the ignition, and with one crank the engine hummed. The air-conditioner kicked in.

It happened so quickly, I could hardly believe it. "Thank you so much," I said several times.

He refused to take any money, smiled, waved, and walked away.

Once I was home, I cancelled the roadside service. "But I didn't thank that wonderful woman at K-Mart," I said out loud to myself. I was so grateful I didn't want to wait another day. I drove back to the store and went inside.

I didn't see her. I described her to the woman at the Customer Service desk, and she didn't know who I meant. I walked up and down the aisles. I went through every department but I couldn't find her.

The next day I returned to K-Mart, but she still wasn't there. Several times over the next week I stopped at different hours, but she was never present. She was never there again with the registers or the layaway or working out on the floor.

I never did find her, and I never saw the helpful mechanic again either.

I cried out to God to forgive me. I had become angry and complained because I couldn't start my car.

"Dear loving God, You and Your angels watched over me."

My husband is in heaven, and I'll see him again. Yet while I'm still on Earth, I know that the Lord is with me. I'm sure that if I need it, He'll send another angel to me, His child. That's just Who God is—a loving, caring Father.

CHAPTER FORTY-ONE

One Cold Night

Susan D. Avery

Things hadn't gone well for us since Bill had been hurt in a car accident. After that, our whole life changed. Yet we were together as a family with three young children. We were a thousand miles from where we started, looking for work and trying to trust God to guide us.

We drove on a bitterly cold night. We had already traveled a long way and were at the end of our money and unsure of the future. Earlier that day we met a really nice man who offered us the use of an empty house.

"You're welcome to stay there for a few months, free of rent," he said.

We were almost there, and I eagerly anticipated getting inside. *At least tonight we'd have a place to stay.* Until we met the man, we were afraid we'd have to sleep in the car.

The man warned us there would be no furniture, no electricity, and no heat. We had candles and what belongings, mostly clothes, we had fit into the trunk of our car.

We unloaded and went into the house. There was one mattress in the front room. We moved it into the center of the house and lit candles. We covered the mattress with a sheet we had in the car so all five of us could lie down to sleep.

The temperature outside was in the single digits, and the wind howled while several inches of new snow fell. Inside, it was warmer, but not much. We piled all our extra clothes on us for warmth. Bill and I took off our coats and spread them out over the children. As we shivered together we began our prayer time with the kids before bedtime.

Before the prayers could begin, however, Michael, our oldest child, said "I'm hungry, And I'm cold."

"So am I," Michelle, our middle child, said.

Our youngest, Meagan, shivered but said nothing.

We pulled them close so that we could share each other's body heat. We had eaten at noon that day, but we had no food to give them.

Bill prayed for all of us, and then I remembered a story that I had read years earlier.

"You children need something to hold on to and to encourage you," I said. "I'd like to tell you a story." I smiled and said, "I've been told it's a true story."

"Is it a good one?" Meagan asked.

"It's a little like our story. It's a story about a family trapped in a blizzard. It happened on Thanksgiving in the mid-1800s."

"The wind howled because there was a raging blizzard that trapped a family of five, and they had no food. They were very hungry and–"

"Like us, huh?" Michael said.

I nodded. "Except worse. It had been a full day since they had eaten. They didn't have anything to drink. Because of the heavy snow they couldn't get to the well for water, so they had to melt snow. The warmth of the fire couldn't keep up with the cold, so they decided to go to bed. Each of the children told their parents how hungry and cold they were–"

"Just like us," Michelle said.

"Their father prayed with them and reassured them that someone would remember them and bring food. The children doubted him because of the blizzard conditions, but he reassured them that someone would, indeed, bring food.

"'What if no one can get through this storm? Will we go hungry?' the oldest child asked.

"'The Lord is going to take care of us. He will find someone to help us.'

"They asked again, 'But what if no one can make it here?'

"The father patiently replied, 'If the Lord can't find anyone to bring us food, He'll bring it Himself!'"

"That's exciting," Michael said. "Just to think that the Lord Himself might bring them something to eat." As he said those words, I knew he was thinking that he wanted God to do that for our family.

"Everyone was snuggled in their beds," I continued, "when there was a sharp knock on the door. The father put on his robe, wondering who could possibly be out in such horrible weather. The children, anticipating food, jumped from their beds and stood behind him when he opened the door.

"A hand held a loaf of bread. That's all. The father took the bread and opened the door wider but he couldn't see anyone. Who had handed him the bread? He looked around but no one was outside.

"'The bread is still hot from the oven,' the wife said as she took it from him.

"The father closed the door and turned around. His eyes lit up and he pointed. 'Look at that!'"

"What was it?" Meagan asked.

"On the table was a bountiful Thanksgiving feast. Everything was warm and freshly prepared. The children asked their father, 'Who brought the food?'

"The father replied, 'I guess the Lord couldn't find anyone to get through the storm, so either He sent an angel with the food or He brought it Himself.'"

By the time I finished telling the story, the children had grown sleepy. Bill reassured them that the Lord would provide for our needs.

"We believe you," Michelle said and so did the other two. They mumbled goodnight and smiled. They truly believed the Lord was going to bring us food as He did that family so long ago.

Bill and I stayed up most of the night, making sure that the children slept and were kept as warm as possible. We finally dozed off in the early morning hours.

A sharp knock at the door awakened Bill and me. He jumped up, ran across the room, and opened the door. "There's no one here," he said.

"Maybe just the wind or something like that," I said.

Bill lay down again. About half an hour later, there was another sharp knock at the door. I looked out of the windows and it was light enough, but I couldn't see anyone outside.

Bill opened the door and again there was no one. He started to close the door. "Susan! Look at this!"

Someone had stacked boxes on top of boxes on the snow-covered porch. I looked around but there were absolutely no footprints in the snow. We could see no evidence of anyone having been there. And yet the boxes were on the porch.

"The Lord either sent an angel or brought them Himself," I said and helped Bill carry the boxes inside.

"There must be enough food for us to live on for a week," Bill said before he praised God.

Minutes later, the children awakened to the smell of food. They hurried to the tables we made out of the boxes. We had hot biscuits and gravy as well as juice and milk. While they ate, Bill and I told them what happened.

"God sure did provide," Meagan said. "And I like everything God gave us."

Two of the boxes contained thermal blankets and candles, and another held cleaning supplies, soap, sponges, paper towels, light bulbs, and even toilet paper. We also received canned goods and a few cooking utensils.

"This is a miracle," Michael said. "It happened just like the story you told us."

"Yes, it did," Bill said, and we hugged each other.

We never did learn who brought the gifts. It was truly a miracle, just like the miracle in the Thanksgiving story I told them the night before. All five of us got down on our knees and thanked our heavenly Father for sending His provision.

Within a week, strangers came to us. They brought us furniture. Others paid for our electricity and heat. Despite our asking, none of them would tell us why they were being so kind or how they learned of our predicament.

Bill found work, and we were able to weather the economic storm in our lives. Other storms would inevitably buffet our lives, but they wouldn't ever have the power to make us question God's provision.

God would take care of us—He had proven that. If He couldn't find someone to be His feet and hands, He would send us an angel or deliver what we needed Himself.

CHAPTER FORTY-TWO

Angels on the Roof: The Story of Clyde Taylor

Carolyn Curtis

The flamboyant Campa and two companions arrived one day while we were building our permanent mission station in Peru. Several inches taller than the other two, he wore a feathered crown and multicolored beads over his *cushma* (a traditional sacklike gown).

From his brightly painted skin and his stiff appearance, I assumed he wanted to impress us with his powerful position of control over the large area around the Amazon River.

We were missionaries in 1926, in an area on the Amazon from which no white person had ever survived. Despite some anxiety because we had heard of the savage Campas, we wanted to be hospitable.

They got out of the canoe and walked toward us. I smiled and welcomed them.

The leader spoke little Spanish, so we communicated with our few common words and gesturing. We offered him food, which he refused. He didn't go inside our hut, but scrutinized the house we were constructing. Each of his aides held up a parrot, and we finally understood he had come to sell them to us. We bartered five yards of red calico for the two birds.

To entertain him, we brought out our Victrola, a crank-powered phonograph and played a record. Although popular in America, the device was a novelty to our Peruvian guests. The machine produced scratchy music, yet it fascinated our visitor. He slowly circled the Victrola, almost reverently, peering at it from every angle.

His face expressed both amusement and wonder. I was relieved to see a human reaction from that potentially violent man. I assumed he was assessing us and trying to decide if we had anything worth looting.

Abruptly he said, "*Adios*," and motioned to his two minions to leave.

Later we learned from the few families who had befriended us that our mysterious visitor was the Campa tribal chief. We hoped we had made the right impression on that powerful warrior and that he would leave us in peace.

They warned us that he boasted he had murdered six missionaries. They also warned us that if the Campas ever attacked, they would come during a full moon.

The significance of the chief's visit became clear a few weeks later. We finished our work just at dusk. The sun sets quickly in that part of the world, and within minutes the full moon shone on the jungle and spread light among the towering trees.

I don't know what alerted me, but I spotted a canoe silently cutting through the water headed downstream toward our compound. One lone Campa paddled the enormous craft, making it obvious to us that other Indians were hiding nearby. While moving with the current, one Indian could steer such a canoe, large enough for fifteen to twenty passengers, but it required six or eight strong men to paddle it upstream.

Where are those other Indians?

A chilling fear raced down my spine. If others were hiding, that meant at least half a dozen armed warriors against my two fellow missionaries and me. I knew we couldn't defend ourselves against them.

Before long, we knew they had come to attack us. An eerie series of whistles filled the night. Those signals, created by whistling through hands cupped over their mouths or by blowing through large snail shells, filled the night air.

We grabbed our rifles and flashlights and headed into the jungle, far enough away to be hidden but close enough to hear the whistles.

They had the reputation of being remarkably accurate with bows and arrows. They scraped tree bark and tied the bark onto the points of their arrows. They set the tips on fire. When they attacked, flaming arrows arced high into the air and pierced the thatched roof of their prey's hut.

Once the building caught fire, they rushed inside, grabbed anything of value and were out before the roof collapsed. If the hut's inhabitants were asleep or caught unaware, the Campas usually killed them.

The whistles continued, but at midnight they intensified. Warriors gathered around our hut.

Then silence. We waited to see the flames destroying our home.

For several minutes nothing happened.

Then noise alerted us of their retreat. I sneaked out of my hiding place and watched them board their huge canoes and paddle away.

Despite our fear of their returning and hordes of mosquitoes attacking us, we spent the night in hiding. They didn't come back, so about daybreak we returned to our compound.

The hut was standing exactly as we had left it. We poked through our belongings. They had taken nothing and, so far as we could see, they hadn't disturbed anything.

After that strange night, we felt safe and never again had to abandon the house in fear.

✦   ✦   ✦   ✦   ✦

Several years later the flamboyant tribal chief became a Christian and called himself Elias.

When he spoke to us about that night, Elias lowered his head, stared at the ground, and said, "We came to attack you." He indicated that he had brought somewhere between thirty and forty Indians.

"Why didn't you attack us?" I asked.

He shook his head. "Too many of you."

"I do not understand," I said.

"Your roof was covered with warriors. We were much afraid," Elias said in halting Spanish. "We could not win against such an army."

I marveled as I listened to Elias describe those warriors whom, he said, wore dazzling white *cushmas*, while the Campas wear only brown.

Not only did the men on the roof wear white, but there were so many of them, he said, "I could not have shot an arrow between them."

God sent His angels to protect us. How else could I explain the incident? Our thatch roof couldn't have held the weight of such a great number of warriors.

That incident reminds me that the Lord provides exactly the kind of provision and protection needed to get His work done.

Not only did God send us angels, but they were dressed in the style of our would-be murderers.

CHAPTER FORTY-THREE

Stand Still

Bonnie Compton Hanson

I let our cat out as usual, but I didn't see her come back in. "Don," I called, "have you seen Calico?"

Our cat loves playing her nightly watch-the-great-lioness-in-action game. Crouched behind a pot of flowers, she stalks her prey—and then she pounces. Her prey isn't ever anything more than a moth or cricket. After she tires of the game, she's ready to leave her wild side and come into our warm, secure, cat-dish-furnished house.

All my life I've loved animals of every description, especially dogs and cats. And they like me in return.

"Have you seen Calico?" I asked again.

My husband glanced up from his book. "I didn't know she'd gone out."

"That's okay. I'll bring her inside."

Outside, a golden moon shimmered against the night sky. Crickets and tree frogs chirped. Somewhere in the distance dogs barked. "Okay, girl," I called, "game's over. Come out of your hiding place and get ready for bed."

Still calling Calico as I looked for her, I walked out to the end of our driveway. Just then, two huge dogs bounded down our street. Obviously they'd slipped off their leashes or broken out of their yards. The two dogs turned and raced into our yard, stopping only inches in front of me. One was a chow; the other, an ugly mixed breed with powerful, rippling muscles.

We have many dogs in our neighborhood, and I love meeting them. I expected those two strangers to wag their tails and whine to be petted, the same way other dogs did around me. Instead, their eyes were glazed and their fangs bared. Both snarled as if ready to leap on top of me.

I froze. Our house was too far away to turn and run inside—as if I could outrun those huge beasts. Our street was deserted. If I turned around, they'd be on my back in an instant. I didn't know what to do. "Dear God, please help me," I prayed silently.

A strong voice called out, "Stare at them! Don't lose control! Stand still and see the deliverance of the Lord!"

I shook so badly, I could hardly keep standing. But that voice filled my heart with calmness. I straightened up and stood still, staring into their faces.

Snarling and snapping, the two dogs suddenly stopped and stared back. Finally, after what seemed like minutes, they turned and headed down the street.

I let out a deep sigh and started to move, but both dogs whirled around and charged right back–leaping up into the air and landing in front of me, even closer than before.

"Stand still!" commanded that same voice.

I was terrified, but I kept standing and staring. I was so terrified I didn't dare blink.

This sounds unbelievable, but they stopped–right in front of me– as if held back by an unseen hand. I was so shocked I couldn't move.

They backed up and lunged again–this time close enough for their spit to spray my face. Again, that same unseen hand held them and kept them from touching me.

I stared at them, and they stared at me. Seconds later, they turned and ran off.

"Thank You, God, for–"

But before I could take a step toward the house those two howling monsters had turned around and charged yet again. This time, with a long, running leap, they hurled themselves at me with all their might.

Again, they were stopped abruptly by that same unseen hand. Snapping and growling, they headed down the street.

This time they didn't return.

Now I understand why Calico had remained hidden. It took me about an hour of coaxing before the frantic cat finally streaked in through our front door. It took that long for my own shakes to subside as well.

To many, my experience seems impossible. It was—and it could never have happened, except that my loving Father took care of me. He did what I couldn't do for myself.

Back inside I told Don what had happened. We'd been married a long time, and he believed me. He shook his head slowly and quoted Psalm 91:11: "For he will order his angels to protect you wherever you go."

As the voice had commanded, I stood still. And I witnessed the deliverance of the Lord.

CHAPTER FORTY-FOUR

Angel in a Maid's Uniform

Sandra P. Aldrich

I'm one of those individuals who locates the emergency doors as soon as I get on the plane—as in *three rows up and to the left*. When I check into a hotel, I make certain of my floor's exit and say to myself, *I'm on the eighth floor, stairs are to the right*. Once I've determined my route of escape if there's an emergency, I settle in for a good flight or go about my normal business.

Throughout their early childhood, my children, Jay and Holly, watched me check exits. They finally spoke up.

They were in their early teens when we traveled to Niagara Falls for a long weekend.

"You need to change your crisis mode of thinking," Jay insisted.

"You're making us crazy," Holly added. "You need to stop being so paranoid."

I assured them I was only being prepared in case something should go wrong.

"Nothing will go wrong," Jay assured me. "Besides, we're with you."

After we registered at our hotel I gave in to their insistence and didn't look for the stairs nearest our room as we unpacked.

Early the next morning, as we prepared to leave for breakfast, the fire alarm went off. Shocked, we stared at one another, hardly believing what we'd heard.

I wanted to wave my arms and yell, "I told you this would happen someday!" But I was the adult and their parent, so with my best imitation of calmness, I said, "Let's just get out of here."

I walked to the door, thankful the handle was cold to my touch, and opened it cautiously. As soon as we left the room, we stepped into a pitch-black hallway. Not even the usual emergency exit lights were visible. I tried to remember which way we had walked down the hallway the night before, but I couldn't recall. Panic almost took over because I had no idea which way to turn for our escape.

"Father God, please help us," I prayed out loud.

Immediately a heavily accented Hispanic woman's voice sounded from the end of the corridor to our right. "Is anyone on this floor?"

"Yes. Three of us."

"You must come this way," she said. "Follow my voice."

With a young Jay and Holly hanging on my left arm and blouse, I felt along the wall with my right hand as we hurried toward the woman. "I hear you coming," she said. "Keep coming this way. Follow my voice."

The three of us didn't say anything as we moved through the darkness. Their hearts probably pounded as hard as mine did.

After what seemed like a long time, we arrived at the stairwell, which was lit by early morning sunlight. The woman, dressed in an old-fashioned black-and-white hotel uniform, stood near the window.

I thanked her repeatedly, but she waved us toward the steps.

"You're okay now," she said. "But hurry."

Once outside, we moved past the fire trucks to stand with the other guests and uniformed staff. We scrutinized the crowd, seeking our benefactor.

She wasn't among those standing outside the hotel. No matter how many times we looked through the crowd, we never saw her again.

Later, we marveled that her voice had called down the corridor the instant I prayed for help.

"I think God sent her," I said to my children.

As I've reflected on the event, I realized God doesn't always send such direct, on-the-spot answers to our prayers. But every now and again God intervenes through messengers—human or heavenly.

CHAPTER FORTY-FIVE

Airplane Angel

Dinorah Cloyd with Lill Kobler

When I was eighteen years old, my father had granted me permission to fly from Mexico City to Des Moines, Iowa, to see my aunt and uncle. It was my first solo trip to the United States.

The year was 1945, and I was excited to make such an adventurous journey. At the time, however, I spoke no English and that worried me. My father's secretary said it wouldn't be a problem for me. She made the flight arrangements.

I was young, eager, and the details of the flight were of little consequence to me. I'd take off, be in the air for a period of time, and then land in Des Moines.

The secretary probably told me and I hadn't listened, because I didn't understand that planes don't always make direct flights to their destination. When I boarded I had no fear about my lack of knowledge of the English language. As far as I was concerned my aunt and uncle would be waiting for me when the plane landed.

Shortly after takeoff I struck up a conversation with the nice-looking man sitting next to me. Although he was obviously an Anglo, he spoke fluent Spanish. I don't remember much of our initial conversation, but one thing stands out. He mentioned that our plane stopped at Fort Worth.

"But I'm not going to Fort Worth," I explained.

"This plane will land at Meacham Airport in Fort Worth," he insisted.

"What must I do when we get there? Is there a plane waiting to take me to Des Moines?"

He shook his head. "You have to take a different plane in Dallas to finish your trip."

His words confused me even more. "You say I must get off the plane in Fort Worth and from there I board a plane in Dallas to get to Iowa. Where is Dallas? How do I get there?" I rattled off the questions as fast as the worries came to me.

"You'll need to take a bus from Fort Worth to Dallas. It's not far."

"Not far? I don't know what that means." I asked him more questions, and he was patient with me.

He smiled at me again. "When we land at Fort Worth, give me your ticket and passport and I'll take care of everything."

How was I going to find the transfer bus? What if I missed the bus and had to find another way to the Dallas airport? What about my luggage? What if I missed my other flight? The more I thought about the situation, the more fearful I became. If I failed in my little adventure I would never be allowed out of the country again without an escort.

The plane landed at Fort Worth, and we got off. Inside the terminal my seat partner pointed toward a chair. "Sit there and wait for me," he said and hurried down the long terminal with dozens of other passengers.

I didn't know where he went. He had my ticket and my passport. I didn't even know his name. What if he didn't come back? What if he left me there?

"Have I done the right thing?" I asked the Lord. I prayed, probably because I didn't know what else do to. I had given my ticket to a stranger. Sitting, waiting, and watching the people hustling about the place, I realized I was lost. If he didn't return—no, I stopped myself from thinking like that. I prayed again.

I opened my eyes, and just like magic, the man from the airplane came toward me. The peaceful smile on his face erased all my fears. "Thank You, Lord," I prayed, "for sending this kind man to me. Now I know I've done the right thing and You're taking care of me."

The man held bus tickets for both of us to ride to the Dallas airport. He walked me to the bus pickup stop, and we waited silently for the bus to arrive. Once we were on board, he spoke words of little consequence, but his kind voice distracted me from worrying.

By the time we arrived at the Dallas airport, I was excitedly ready to continue the adventure. As I stepped off the bus, once again everything looked foreign to me. Locating my next flight wouldn't be easy. The airports of today bring the plane up to the terminal, but back then we walked out onto the tarmac to the plane. I had to know which plane to board and, with no knowledge of English, I didn't know whom or how to ask.

Over the PA system, a voice announced flights and gates, and even though I could hear, the words went by too quickly for me to grasp. I stood there, listening and quietly praying for guidance.

"This way," the man I'd met on the other plane said in Spanish. He gently placed a hand on my elbow and guided me out the door. He pointed to my airplane, where passengers had lined up. He walked to the end of the line with me, checked to make certain I had my ticket. "I must be going," he said and smiled. "You'll be all right now." He held out his hand.

"Thank you so much for what you have done for me today." I held his hand tightly. "I cannot tell you how much it means to me." As I said those words, I realized he had something clasped in his hand. "What is this?"

He opened his hand, exposing a golden coin. On the coin was one word, *Dinorah*.

"That's *my* name. How did you know my name?" I hadn't introduced myself.

"I was here to take care of you." He flipped the coin over showing the name Olga written on the other side. "Now, I'm going to take care of Olga." He bowed his head slightly, turned away, and left.

I lost sight of him before he reached the terminal door. The remainder of my trip my mind was so filled with what happened, I forgot my excitement about being in the United States.

My luggage arrived on the same flight. I had no problems on the flight back to Mexico City.

✦ ✦ ✦ ✦ ✦

That day, on my first visit to the United States, I learned one of the most valuable lessons of my life. God cares about me and is always there to help. Even before I knew I was going to need help, God had already sent someone to come to my aid.

And not just anyone, but an angel whose day wasn't done. He still had to help Olga.

Surely that's what the prophet meant when he wrote, "I will answer them before they even call to me. While they are still talking about their needs, I will go ahead and answer their prayers!" (Isaiah 65:24).

CHAPTER FORTY-SIX

"Go Back to Sleep, Sis"

Marley Gibson

Cancer. Cancer is one of those words my grandmother used to whisper–like *prison* or *divorce*. Those were words she couldn't bring herself to say out loud at the dinner table or in mixed company.

Cancer.

It's something I used to think about happening to people I don't know. Or the elderly. Or sad little children with their pictures on billboards. Stories I read about for fund-raisers, or walkathons, or saw on TV reports.

I never thought my grandmother would whisper the word *cancer* in reference to me.

But there I was in the summer of 1982, age fifteen, and a newly named varsity cheerleader going into my sophomore year of high school with a driver's permit in my wallet. That's when I was diagnosed with periosteal osteosarcoma. No matter what the medical professionals termed it with their words that were seemingly filled with more vowels than consonants, it came down to only one thing: I had cancer.

I don't remember the exact moment that my teenaged brain—focused on thoughts of cheerleading, boys, and summer—fully grasped the reality of what was happening to me. I think being shuffled through the offices of countless doctors and hospital exam rooms would have spelled it out easily. Perhaps the full body scans and X-rays at every angle should have slammed me into reality. Or the CT scan, followed by an arteriogram. Not even the hot dye surging through my veins made me realize the severity of what was going on in my adolescent body.

It wasn't because I was naïve or ignorant. After all, I was a member of the National Honor Society. It wasn't denial either. It was that as I lay in the hospital bed day after day, I constantly thought about cheering for the first football game.

Being a varsity cheerleader was a finally realized dream. Since elementary school I had dreamed of being a cheerleader. I wanted to be on the sidelines cheering on the football team, doing cartwheels, and hoisting my partner up for stunts and pyramids.

I didn't care about the myriad tests and X-rays run on me on a daily basis. I just wanted to get the "hospital stuff" over with so I could pick up my pompoms and get into uniform.

I didn't know what was going on behind the scenes, of course. Every day, my mother talked to the doctors and nurses and got as much information as possible. She slept in a reclining chair in my room every night. My father drove up every weekend to see us. My cheerleading squad voted whether to keep me on the team–which they did–thanks to an impassioned plea from my mother not to take the position away from me. However, I didn't know any of that as I went through two biopsies on my left leg to determine what the mass was around my fibula.

"Your tumor isn't really an apple or an orange," the doctor said one day. "It's sort of a fruit salad."

"What does that mean?" I asked.

The doctor looked from my parents to me. "The tumor is benign toward the outside of your leg. However, it's malignant on the inside, closer to your tibia."

That didn't sound good.

"I'll have to remove the fibula, the tumor, and part of the periosteal nerve, but if the cancer has reached the tibia, we'll have to explore our options. We won't know until we operate." He shook his head and said, "I've never seen a cancer like this before."

Great, I can't have some common cancer like other people, I thought. I have to have a landmark case that would eventually get my doctor written up in *Cancer* magazine.

The word *malignant* echoed in my head and began to conjure up bad things. Surgery. Bone and nerve removal. Chemo. Radiation. Loss of appetite. Loss of hair. Never walking again. This had become a lot more serious than "just cut it out and send me back to school."

It meant an eight-hour surgery to determine the extent of the cancer's journey in my body. It meant the possibility of my coming out of it short one limb.

The night before my "big surgery"–as I like to call it–my mother and I were awakened by a visitor in my room. She was a rotund, African American woman, dressed in white, and she stood at the foot of my bed. With her hand gently placed on my left leg, she closed her eyes and moved her lips in prayer.

"Is everything okay?" Mother asked in her sleep-haze.

"Go back to sleep, Sis," the woman said sweetly to her. Then she looked at me and said, "Everything's going to be fine. God has plans for you."

With that, the kind woman left the room, and Mother and I went back to sleep.

The next day, Mother went to the nurses' station to seek the woman out and thank her for praying for me. However, there was no one working that fit her description. There wasn't anyone on the shifts before, during, or after who had seen her either.

One nurse finally said, "Oh, you saw her too."

"Too?" we asked.

"She's not a nurse at this hospital." Before we could say anything she added, "A lot of people have reported seeing her before their surgeries. We think she's an angel."

Mother and I gripped hands, knowing that she indeed was an angel sent to comfort and reassure us in our darkest hour.

Shortly thereafter, my mother read me a Bible verse, "My help cometh from the Lord, which made heaven and earth. He will not suffer thy foot to be moved" (Psalm 121:2–3).

✦ ✦ ✦ ✦ ✦

The surgery went well, the tumor was removed, and my leg was saved. I had three weeks of chemotherapy and radiation. I returned to school with an ACE bandage covering my scar and crutches to help me walk.

I put on my uniform and cheered. Soon, because of the chemo, my waist-length hair fell out, but I approached my baldness with humor. The football team shaved their heads that year, thinking it would make them look tough. Rival schools merely thought I had *that* much school spirit as well.

My visiting angel was right. Everything was fine.

And the woman who came into my room was right: God had plans for me.

But for me, it's more than a story about my recovery. In addition to sharing my experience in a fictional book, I have started a nonprofit charity called The Radiate Foundation for young adults currently in the hospital undergoing cancer treatment, www.radiatefoundation.org. Just as God and His angel were with my family and me that summer, I want The Radiate Foundation to bring as much hope, joy, and cheer to others.

Whenever life's stresses or disappointments get me down, I remember the angel's voice to my mother and to me. "Go back to sleep, Sis. Everything's going to be fine."

And it always is.

WHO WE ARE

CECIL MURPHEY is the author or coauthor of more than 125 books, including the best sellers *90 Minutes in Heaven* (with Don Piper) and *Gifted Hands* (with Ben Carson, MD). His books have sold millions of copies and have brought hope and encouragement to countless readers around the world. Find him online at www.cecilmurphey.com.

TWILA BELK, aka the Gotta Tell Somebody Gal, is a Christian communicator who loves to brag on God. She works full time with veteran author Cecil Murphey and enjoys speaking, writing, and teaching at writers' conferences. *Because You Care*, her coauthored book with Cecil Murphey, was released in 2012. Visit Twila at www.gottatellsomebody.com.

SANDY ADAMS has enjoyed writing, speaking to women's groups, and teaching marriage seminars for more than twenty years. She and her husband of thirty-nine years reside in Georgetown, Texas. She has one son and four grandchildren. Sandy's passion is in finding and sharing the beauty and joy of each new day. Contact her at sandyadams@onemain.com.

NANCY AGUILAR is a freelance writer and editor whose writing has appeared in *Mature Years*, *The Best of Proverbs 31*, *Vista*, and the worship CD *Hideaway*. She has two sons and lives in Lake Forest Park, Washington, where she and her husband enjoy scenic runs together. Contact Nancy at njaguilar@comcast.net.

SANDRA P. ALDRICH, president and CEO of Bold Words, Inc. in Colorado Springs, Colorado, is an award-winning author and international speaker. She has written or cowritten nineteen books and is a contributor to two dozen more. Her Web site is www.sandraaldrich.com.

GLORIA ASHBY is a speaker, teacher, and writer whose published works appear in *Chicken Soup for the Soul*, *Love Is a Verb Devotional*, *Secret Place*, and local communications. She lives in Texas with her husband Jim and enjoys reading and digging in her butterfly garden. Find Gloria's weekly blog, *Glimpses of God*, at www.gloriaashby.wordpress.com.

SUSAN D. AVERY, a freelance writer, is working toward a future in curriculum development in religious education. She writes for magazines and does copyediting, ghostwriting, and performs other writing and print services. Susan and her husband Bill cofounded Bluesun Ministries. Visit her Web site at www.bluesunministries.com/Susan-Avery.html.

ELIZABETH BAKER is an author and retired counselor, drawing on thirty-five years of experience to help individuals apply biblical principles to real-life situations. She currently lives in Pittsburg, Texas, where she concentrates on her writing. A widow since her midthirties, Elizabeth has four grown children, fifteen grandchildren, and six great grandchildren. www.ElizabethBakerBooks.com

GRACE G. BOOTH is a retired teacher and a freelance writer who's published in numerous periodicals and book anthologies including *Guideposts*. She leads the Royal Writers group in Picayune, Mississippi, and codirects the Southern Christian Writers Guild in Mandeville, Louisiana. Contact Grace at Ruwriting2@yahoo.com.

MARY CANTELL says that when a third-grade teacher told her parents their daughter would never become a mathematician, signs pointed to a creative world. In carrying out the self-fulfilling prophecy, she became a news broadcaster, columnist, and voice artist. She hopes to market her first novel, *Her Glass Heart*, soon. Visit her at www.marycantell.com.

ELLEN CARDWELL is a native Californian, recently transplanted from the Bay Area to the Sierra Nevada foothills. She began her writing career with devotionals. She also writes longer pieces. Visit www.ellencardwell.net to read some of her stories.

DINORAH CLOYD is an accomplished artist who has traveled frequently throughout her life. She's willing to share stories about God working with her through her experiences. Her love of reading led her to encourage others to write.

BETTY CORNETT and her husband Timothy have pastored three churches and traveled together in ministry for the past forty-eight years in more than eighty-six countries. In 1988, they made their first trip to Eastern Europe, where they found a "second home" in Bulgaria. Betty loves missions, music, teaching, and any position in which God allows her to serve. www.cornettministries.com

CAROLYN CURTIS is an award-winning article writer, book author and collaborator, corporate and ministry publications editor, and speaker at writers' conferences. She holds bachelor of arts and master's degrees in journalism. Her work has appeared in publications ranging from *The Saturday Evening Post* to *Sports Illustrated* to *Christianity Today*. www.carolyncurtis.net

PAMELA DOWD, a multipublished author, enjoys writing family stories, novels, greeting cards, articles, and devotionals. Her daily inspiration and storytelling fodder springs from intimate relationships with God, her husband, three daughters, three sons-in-law, six grandchildren, elderly parents, and dear friends. www.pameladowd.com

SANDEE MARTIN DRAKE, a retired French and Spanish high school teacher, loves to ski, quilt, knot, read, and write. One of her stories appears in the book *Tales from H.E.L. and Beyond*. Her first novel is completed, and she looks forward to seeing it published. Contact her at sandeedrake@outdrs.net.

Margee Dyck and her husband Arthur retired to Oregon after thirty-eight years of ministry in Canada. They have four sons and ten grandchildren. Margee has written an award-winning children's television series, children's books, articles, church programs, dramas, and a novel. E-mail her at artmargedyck@hotmail.com.

Terri Elders, LCSW, lives near Colville, Washington, with two dogs and three cats. Her stories are widely published, including in a dozen *Chicken Soup for the Soul* anthologies. She's a public member of the Washington State Medical Quality Assurance Commission. She blogs at www.atouchoftarragon.blogspot.com. Write her at telders@hotmail.com.

Virginia Garberding is a registered nurse with more than twenty-five years of experience in the field of geriatric nursing. Virginia co-authored *Please Get to Know Me: Aging with Dignity and Relevance* with Cecil Murphey. On her blog at www.nursevirginiablog.com, she provides healthcare information for caregivers.

DiAne Gates writes and illustrates for children, leads a writers' group for North Texas Christian Writers, and facilitates

GriefShare. Her books include *Arnold the Ant* and *Roped*. Her devotionals have appeared in *The Secret Place*. She is writing a devotional series for the family, *The Master's Plan*. E-mail her at dianegates@sbcglobal.net.

MARLEY GIBSON is a multipublished young-adult author. Her book *Radiate* (Houghton Mifflin Harcourt) is a fictionalized version of her battle with cancer while a teenage cheerleader. She also coauthored *Christmas Miracles* and *The Spirit of Christmas* (St. Martin's Press) with Cecil Murphey. Find her online at www.marleygibson. com, on Facebook www.facebook.com/marley.h.gibson, or Twitter @MarleyGibson.

JEAN MATTHEW HALL is a freelance writer whose stories and articles appear in a variety of inspirational magazines and anthologies. She is the cofounder and conference coordinator for the Write2Ignite! Conference for Christian writers (www.write2ignite.com). Contact Jean at www.jeanmatthewhall.com or www.jeanmatthewhallwords. blogspot.com.

BONNIE COMPTON HANSON, an artist and speaker, is the author of more than thirty books for adults and children, plus hundreds of articles, stories, and poems (including thirty-three for *Chicken Soup for the Soul*). A former editor, she's also taught at several universities and writers' conferences. www.bonniecomptonhanson.com

LORI HINTERMEISTER, married to her high school sweetheart Gary for thirty-one years, is the mother of three children and the proud grandmother of a new grandson. She enjoys her job as secretary for a local elementary school. Lori's e-mail is bettlah@aol.com.

HELEN L. HOOVER enjoys sewing, knitting, reading, and traveling. Her devotionals and personal stories appear in five books and various denominations' handouts. She and her husband Larry volunteer with the Sower Ministry for retired RVers. Their life is blessed with two children, four grandchildren, and three great-grandchildren. E-mail her at lnhhoover@yahoo.com.

DEBBIE JOHNSON is a student of the Bible, past Sunday school teacher, and administrator at an electric cooperative. She lives in East Texas with her husband Johnny. Debbie enjoys reading, but her greatest joys in life are her two children and nine grandchildren.

KAREN BARNES JORDAN is best known for telling the stories that matter most. She has multiple writing credits and trains other writers as well. Karen and her husband Dan reside in Hot Springs Village, Arkansas, near their two children and seven grandchildren. Contact Karen at kj@karenjordan.net or visit www.karenjordan.net.

KATHLEEN KOHLER is a writer and speaker from the Pacific Northwest. Her articles, rooted in personal experience, appear in books and magazines. She and her husband have three children and seven grandchildren. Kathleen enjoys gardening, travel, and watercolor painting. Visit www.KathleenKohler.com to read more of her published work.

LILL KOHLER, daughter of Dinorah Cloyd, inherited Dinorah's love of travel and seeing God's hand at work. When she's not out on the road with her husband, she's planning her next blog posting for www.rocking-myworld.blogspot.com.

DELILAH MOORE LEACH earned a bachelor's degree in English from Northwest Nazarene College and a master's degree from Western Oregon. She taught high school for twenty-nine years before having to quit for health reasons. She lives with her husband Jeff in Lebanon, Oregon. Find more about Delilah at www.delilahmooreleach.tateauthor.com.

JEFFREY LEACH graduated from Northwest University with a bachelor's degree in biblical literature, used his musical talents to help local churches, and pastored in the Northwest. He raised two daughters with his wife Delilah. Jeff loves bow hunting and salmon fishing and uses the sports as ministry outlets. Jeff's e-mail is jdleach48@comcast.net.

PATRICIA LEE has several nonfiction articles published in magazines and is working toward publication of her first novel. She lives with her husband Loren in Springfield, Oregon. They have two grown children and four cats. Patricia blogs at www.patriciaponders. wordpress.com. Her Web site is www.patricialeewrites.com.

HEATHER MARSTEN is writing a memoir about healing from abuse and the occult. She is a happily married mom of three grown children. Contact her at heathermarsten@gmail.com or visit her blogs at www.xanga.com/wondering04 (Bible studies) and www.heathermarsten.wordpress.com (healing from abuse).

ANDREA ARTHUR OWAN is an educator, writer, and speaker. She is the mother of three children. Andrea lives in Tucson, Arizona, with her husband and their youngest child, the boy in her story. Contact her at alaowan@comcast.net.

ELISE DALY PARKER and her husband of twenty-seven years are parents to four daughters. A writer and editor for more than twenty-five years in advertising, marketing, and magazine publishing, she invites you to join her at www.OurStoriesGodsGlory.blogspot.com. Find out more at www.EliseDalyParker.com.

EDWINA PERKINS is a writer, teacher, missionary, and speaker. She's a contributor to *Christmas Miracles* and serves as president of the Orlando chapter of Word Weavers. Edwina lives with her family in central Florida where she's at work on her second novel. You can reach her via e-mail at perkster6@earthlink.net.

Roy Peterson, president and CEO since 2003 of The Seed Company, a Wycliffe Bible Translators affiliate, served as president and CEO of Wycliffe USA from 1997 until 2003, after ministering for Wycliffe in Ecuador and Guatemala. Roy and his wife Rita live in Dallas. They have three children and three grandchildren. Visit www.theseedcompany.org for more information.

Wes Peterson spent his childhood in Ecuador and Guatemala as a missionary kid. He and his wife Jama have served the Lord together since 1999 on staff at local churches and through mission organizations. Wes currently works as a ministry coach through Commission to Every Nation and is an executive pastor in Arlington, Texas. His e-mail is wespeterson@gmail.com.

Don Piper has shared his story of death—and life—with more than three thousand audiences around the world. He's also reached millions through TV, radio, and print media. He coauthored the best seller *90 Minutes in Heaven* and three other books with Cecil Murphey. Learn more at www.donpiperministries.com.

Colleen L. Reece learned to read by kerosene lamplight in a home that was once a one-room schoolhouse where her mother taught all eight grades. There Colleen dreamed of someday writing a book. God has expanded her dream into more than 140 "Books You Can Trust," with six million copies sold. E-mail Colleen at colleenreece@q.com.

SHIRLEY A. REYNOLDS is a freelance writer living in a rural mountain community in Idaho. Her favorite things include riding her ATV on the back roads, hiking, photography, and writing from her loft overlooking the Sawtooth Mountains. Reach her at heartprints@ netzero.net.

JANICE RICE is passionate about living out her Christian walk as an adventure. She has worked as a youth pastor, started new churches, and led numerous mission trips to Mexico and Fiji. Janice's degree is in cross-cultural communications. She currently pastors with her husband and four children in Oregon. Contact her at janice.riverside@hotmail.com.

ELISE DOUGLASS SCHNEIDER, PHD, is an international speaker and author whose many publications include contributions to Guideposts Books and *Focus on the Family*. Her higher-education profession includes two community college presidencies. She's a frequent radio and television guest and serves on the CLASSEMINARS Advisory Board. Visit her Web site at www.eliseschneider.com.

DONNA SHERER treasures any opportunity to share her love for Jesus and the things she has learned on her walk as a Christian.

Donna has been married to Kevin for twenty-five years, and is the mother of three children. She invites you to reach her at sherer.donna@gmail.com.

MARY SALISBURY SKEENS is a seventy-nine-year-old widow who resides in Central Florida. Before migrating from Maryland twenty-two years ago, she earned an associate's degree and attended Rollings College in Winter Park, where she majored in English and psychology. Since retiring in 1999, she enjoys writing for Christian publications. Contact her at OrangeCity32@aol.com.

CATHY TAYLOR is the Women's Ministry Leader at Calvary Fellowship in Mountlake Terrace, Washington, where her husband Wayne is pastor. She has a heart for visiting the sick, sharing her story, and encouraging others. Cathy's the mother of four children and the joyful grandmother of Aurelia. Contact her at cathyt@calvaryfellowship.org.

SONYA LEE THOMPSON is an inspirational writer and speaker whose articles have appeared in many publications such as *Standard* and *The Voice of Grace and Truth*. Living in Virginia with her husband and six children, she facilitates a women's Bible study and leads an MIT group. Visit her at www.sonyaleethompson.com.

RENAE TOLBERT lives in Redding, California. Her publishing credits include *Cup of Comfort for Christian Women* and *Birds and Blooms* magazine, and she's a regular contributor to the *Redding Christian Quarterly* magazine. She's married to Herb, who serves as vice president of enrollment at Simpson University. Her e-mail is Tolbert7@aol.com.

WENDY TOLIVER is the author of several young-adult novels, nonfiction books, short stories, and articles. She writes, edits, teaches writing, and coaches basketball, as well as wakeboards and snowboards, in scenic Eden, Utah, where every day is a new adventure with her husband and three young sons. Visit her at www.wendytoliver.com.

DELORES E. TOPLIFF is a freelance writer, teacher, and speaker with more than 240 publications. Besides teaching at Northwestern College, St. Paul, Minnesota, she presents seminars and is president of the 430-member Minnesota Christian Writers Guild. She provides writing-editing consulting through Creative Design Services, and operates TrueNorth Publishing: A Friend to Writers. www.delorestopliff.com

GENI J. WHITE, a retired psychiatric registered nurse, thanks the Lord for letting her publish hundreds of book reviews while fighting fatigue from the radiation and chemotherapy that killed her colon cancer. (See www.samcivy.wordpress.com.) She writes humor at www.ennabushay.wordpress.com. Geni and Bob, her husband of fifty three years, have three adult children and one daughter-in-law.

JoAnn Reno Wray offers services in writing, editing, and graphic art through her company EpistleWorks Creations (www .epistleworks.com) in Broken Arrow, Oklahoma. With more than three thousand items published in print and Web periodicals, her stories also appear in many compilation books. JoAnn is also a speaker and conference teacher.

A NOTE FROM THE EDITORS

We hope you enjoy *Heavenly Company* by Cecil Murphey with Twila Belk, published by Guideposts Books and Inspirational Media. In all of our books, magazines and outreach efforts, we aim to deliver inspiration and encouragement, help you grow in your faith, and celebrate God's love in every aspect of your daily life.

Thank you for making a difference with your purchase of this book, which helps fund our many outreach programs to the military, prisons, hospitals, nursing homes and schools. To learn more, visit GuidepostsFoundation.org.

We also maintain many useful and uplifting online resources. Visit Guideposts.org to read true stories of hope and inspiration, access OurPrayer network, sign up for free newsletters, join our Facebook community, and follow our stimulating blogs.

To order your favorite Guideposts publications, go to ShopGuideposts.org, call (800) 932-2145 or write to Guideposts, PO Box 5815, Harlan, Iowa 51593.